CHRONOLO

1644

19 January Scots Army led by Earl of Leven invades England

19 March Royalist uprising in Scotland begins, led by Marquis of Huntly

13 April Marquis of Montrose leads English Royalist army north to Dumfries

20 April Montrose flees back to England pursued by Earl of Callendar

29 April Huntly's Royalists evacuate Aberdeen and disperse

27 June Alasdair MacColla's Irish mercenaries sail from Passage near Waterford

8 July Irish land at Ardnamurchan

29 August Montrose is joined by MacColla and again raises the Royal Standard, this time at Blair Castle

1 September Montrose defeats Lord Elcho at Tibbermore, outside Perth

13 September Montrose defeats Lord Balfour of Burleigh at Aberdeen

28 October Indecisive engagement between Montrose and Marquis of Argyle at Fyvie Castle

13 December Royalists seize Inverary

1645

2 February Montrose defeats Argyle at Inverlochy

9 February Lord Gordon defects to the Royalists with a regular cavalry regiment

15 March Sir John Hurry successfully raids Royalist-held Aberdeen

4 April Montrose successfully storms Dundee but is summarily chased out again by Baillie and Hurry

9 May Battle of Auldearn. Montrose defeats Hurry

2 July Montrose defeats Lieutenant-General William Baillie at Alford

15 August Montrose again defeats Baillie at Kilsyth

13 September Major-General David Leslie defeats Montrose at Philiphaugh, near Selkirk.

1646

5 May King Charles I surrenders to the Scots army outside Newark, England

14 May Huntly storms Aberdeen

30 July Montrose disbands his army at Rattray, near Blairgowrie and flees abroad

OPPOSING COMMANDERS

THE ROYALISTS

Ironically enough **James Graham, Marquis of Montrose** (1612–50), first came to prominence as one of the more militant supporters of the National Covenant and only defected to the King's party as the result of political infighting. While this cost him a spell in prison it did not prevent him from being offered a command in the Scots Army in 1643, but instead he rode south to join the King at Oxford. Assessments of Montrose's abilities tend to be excessively coloured by the heroic account of his campaigns – effectively a ghosted autobiography – written by his personal chaplain, George Wishart. A more balanced appreciation raises some serious questions. There is no doubt whatsoever that he was handsome, charming, intellectually gifted and charismatic – the very epitome of the dashing cavalier – or of his dogged determination in the face of adversity. These are all excellent qualities in a general, but all too often that determination bordered on a single-minded fanaticism, which alienated as many potential supporters as it attracted. Worse still it blinded him to the necessities of proper intelligence-gathering, reconnaissance and, indeed, just about every other practical aspect of the soldier's trade. Ultimately this would contribute directly to his defeat at Philiphaugh and the yet more disastrous debacle at Carbisdale in 1650.

Indeed, this neglect very nearly resulted in defeat at Auldearn, but there, as on so many other occasions, it was averted by his major-general, **Alasdair MacColla**. The eldest son of Coll MacDonald of Colonsay, whose nickname *Coll Coitach* (or *Colkitto*) he often shares, he was a professional soldier. He had fought on both sides (twice) in the bloody Irish rebellion before being given command of Antrim's mercenaries and sent to Scotland. Often portrayed as a stout but not overly intelligent foil to Montrose's brilliance, he was actually a very capable soldier. His only real 'failing' lay in his seizing the opportunity opened by the campaign to set himself up as an independent warlord and embark upon a doomed attempt to unite the Western Clans and re-establish Clan Donald's hegemony in the Isles. In May 1647 David Leslie caught up with him in Kintyre and although he fled to Ireland he was killed there at the battle of Knocknanus, near Mallow, on 12 November that year.

THE COVENANTERS

Initially the rebels had the great good fortune to face a succession of political appointees who had sufficient ability to raise troops, but who lacked the skill to employ them properly. Recognising this the government recalled **Lieutenant-General William Baillie** from service in England and

This piper's buff coat suggests that he may be a professional soldier, perhaps serving with Sir Mungo Campbell of Lawers' Regiment at Auldearn.

Auldearn 1645

The Marquis of Montrose's
Scottish campaign

Campaign · 123

OSPREY
PUBLISHING

Auldearn 1645

The Marquis of Montrose's Scottish campaign

Stuart Reid · Illustrated by Gerry Embleton

Series editor Lee Johnson · Consultant editor David G Chandler

First published in Great Britain in 2003 by Osprey Publishing, Elms Court, Chapel Way, Botley, Oxford OX2 9LP, United Kingdom.
Email: info@ospreypublishing.com

A CIP catalogue record for this book is available from the British Library

ISBN 1 84176 679 8

Editor: Lee Johnson
Design: The Black Spot
Index by Alison Worthington
Maps by The Map Studio
3D bird's-eye views by the Black Spot
Battlescene artwork by Gerry Embleton

Originated by The Electronic Page Company, Cwmbran, UK
Printed in China through World Print Ltd.

03 04 05 06 07   10 9 8 7 6 5 4 3 2 1

For a catalogue of all books published by Osprey Military and Aviation please contact:

Osprey Direct UK, P.O. Box 140, Wellingborough,
Northants, NN8 2FA, UK
E-mail: info@ospreydirect.co.uk

Osprey Direct USA, c/o MBI Publishing, P.O. Box 1,
729 Prospect Ave, Osceola, WI 54020, USA
E-mail: info@ospreydirectusa.com

www.ospreypublishing.com

Author's note

The Civil War in Scotland was in reality a Royalist rebellion against the country's legitimate government, and the armies that fought against Montrose were in the service of their country rather than the forces of a mere faction. Nevertheless, both convenience and convention make it easier to loosely refer to them as 'Covenanters'.

Whilst every effort has been made in the orders of battle to identify all of the units present on both sides, no muster rolls survive and in all too many cases it is necessary to extrapolate the numbers serving in individual units from very broad total figures. Those numbers quoted are for the most part therefore approximate estimates that chiefly serve to give a sense of the relative sizes of the various units present.

Artist's note

Readers may care to note that the original paintings from which the colour plates in this book were prepared are available for private sale. All reproduction copyright whatsoever is retained by the Publishers. All enquiries should be addressed to:

Scorpio Gallery,
PO Box 475,
Hailsham,
East Sussex
BN27 2SL
UK

The Publishers regret that they can enter into no correspondence upon this matter.

KEY TO MILITARY SYMBOLS

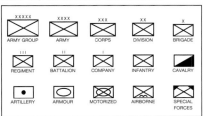

CONTENTS

SCOTLAND IN THE CIVIL WARS

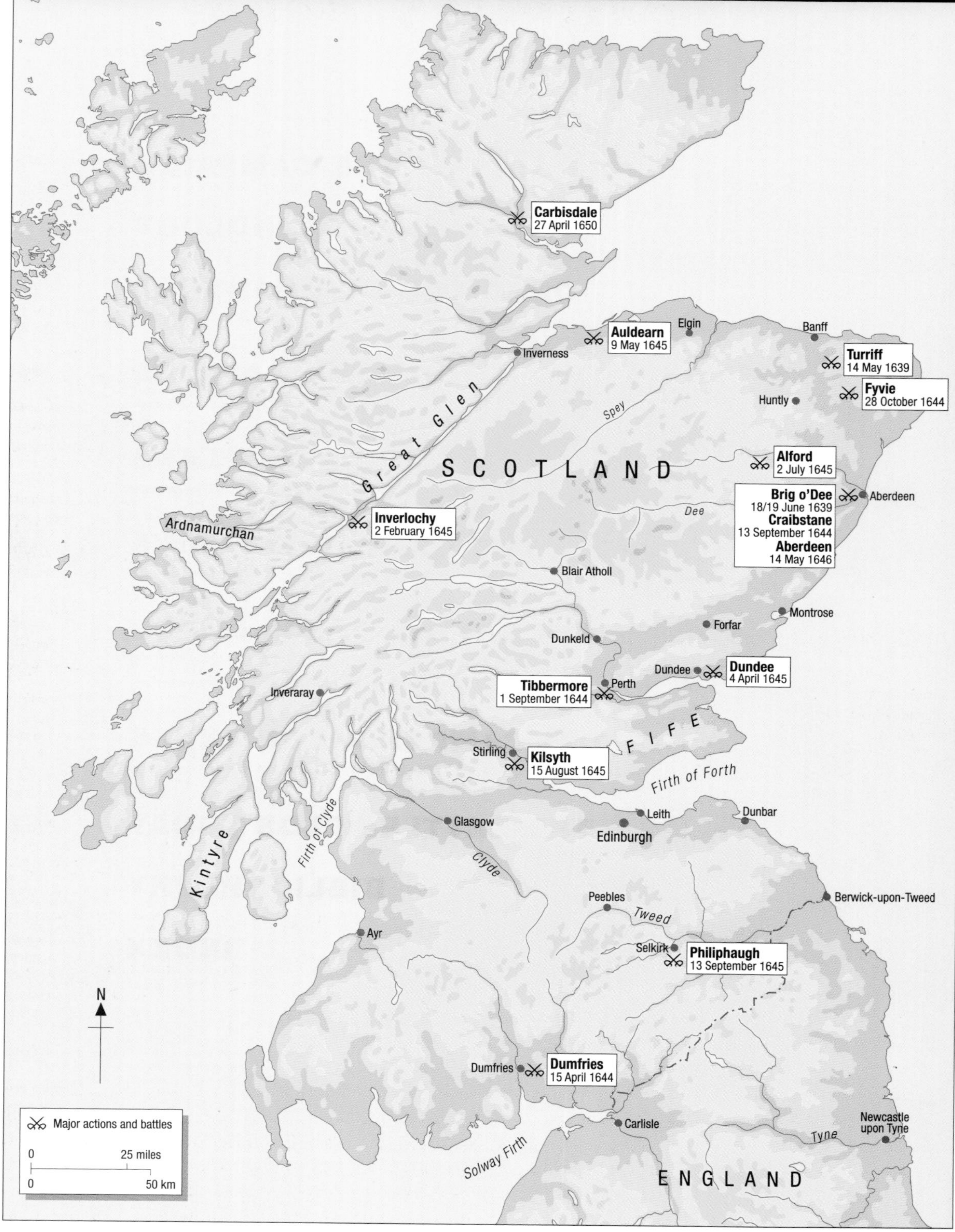

Carbisdale
27 April 1650
Auldearn
9 May 1645
Elgin
Banff
Turriff
14 May 1639
Fyvie
28 October 1644
Inverness
Huntly
Spey
Great Glen
SCOTLAND
Alford
2 July 1645
Brig o'Dee
18/19 June 1639
Craibstane
13 September 1644
Aberdeen
14 May 1646
Aberdeen
Dee
Ardnamurchan
Inverlochy
2 February 1645
Blair Atholl
Montrose
Forfar
Dunkeld
Dundee
Dundee
4 April 1645
Perth
Tibbermore
1 September 1644
Inveraray
FIFE
Stirling
Kilsyth
15 August 1645
Firth of Forth
Leith
Dunbar
Glasgow
Edinburgh
Firth of Clyde
Kintyre
Clyde
Peebles
Tweed
Berwick-upon-Tweed
Ayr
Selkirk
Philiphaugh
13 September 1645
N
Dumfries
Dumfries
15 April 1644
Major actions and battles
0
25 miles
0
50 km
Carlisle
Newcastle upon Tyne
Tyne
Solway Firth
ENGLAND

ORIGINS OF THE CAMPAIGN

James Graham, Marquis of Montrose. Initially an adherent of the Covenant he afterwards changed sides and, making common cause with the Catholic Earl of Antrim, he led a pro-Royalist uprising in a remarkable year-long campaign.

Scotland in the 17th century was an independent country whose king quite fortuitously happened to be King of England as well. From choice Charles I based himself in his richer southern kingdom and took little interest in Scots affairs until his belated coronation in 1633. A slow but steady slide into disaster followed. Two generations before, Scotland had firmly embraced the Protestant Reformation and in particular the teachings of John Calvin, but now the King, having remembered the existence of his northern kingdom, decided to remodel the Scots Kirk on Episcopalian or High Anglican lines. Quite literally smelling as it did of Popish incense this proposal was unpopular enough in itself, but worse was to come. In order to finance both the ecclesiastical reforms, and in particular the hierarchy of bishops that was to replace the democratic Presbyterian system, Charles also proposed to re-possess the former landholdings of the Catholic church. As in England, at the Reformation these vast lands had originally fallen to the Crown and then been sold on to the great benefit of the Exchequer. Now they were to revert to the Crown and although compensation was promised, the state was all but bankrupt and this was widely regarded as unlikely to materialise. Moreover in a culture where the number of a man's tenants was accounted of more worth than more material indicators of wealth, the potential loss of those tenants was a serious matter indeed. The result was that the proposed reforms not only alienated the Protestant population at large, but by directly threatening the wealth and above all the power of the nobility, they also provided the discontented with leaders.

In 1638 a National Covenant was widely signed throughout the country, pledging a substantial part of the population, great and small, to oppose the King's reforms. In 1639 and 1640 two brief and inglorious wars saw King Charles defeated and Scotland's independence very firmly re-asserted. From then onwards although lip-service was still paid to the King as the titular head of state, Scotland was a republic in all but name, and it was as a sovereign power that her government agreed to support the Westminster Parliament in the English Civil War that followed soon afterwards. Under the terms of the Solemn League and Covenant of 1643 Scotland was committed to enter that war with an army of over 20,000 men. Intervention on such a scale would be fatal to the English Royalist cause and so at Oxford an ambitious plan was set in train to knock Scotland back out of the war before it was too late.

There were three main elements to this plan. James Graham, Marquis of Montrose, himself a former Covenanter, was to lead a motley collection of Scots mercenaries and English levies northwards across the border from Carlisle to raise a rebellion in the old Catholic south-west. In the north-east of Scotland the long time Royalist George Gordon, Marquis of Huntly, was to lead a similar rebellion, while in the west

Randal McDonnell, Earl of Antrim, was pledged to bring an army across from Ireland. What was more, and quite unbeknown to most of those involved, the garrison of Stirling Castle, traditionally the key to Scotland, was also disaffected and ready to go over to the rebels as soon as they appeared.

None of the rebels did appear, however. Huntly duly raised his followers as promised and took over Aberdeen, but the Irish never came and Montrose, having arrived rather too late on the scene, briefly occupied Dumfries before being ignominiously chased back across the border considerably quicker than he had come. The garrison of Stirling prudently sat tight, their putative treachery undiscovered, but Huntly, left isolated and alone, was forced to flee for his life and ever afterwards considered himself betrayed by Montrose. In any event it was all in vain. Montrose rode south to beg more men from the King's nephew, Prince Rupert, but on 2 July 1644 the English Royalists' northern army was smashed by an Anglo-Scots army on Marston Moor outside York and Montrose slipped home to Scotland without a single man at his back.

Although Maclan used this figure to represent the Fergusons, it is very largely based on 16th-century illustrations of Irish swordsmen. Nevertheless, there is some evidence to suggest that yellow shirts of this kind were also worn by Scots Highland leaders.

assigned the job of dealing with the rebels to his professional hands. A very competent soldier, Baillie performed rather better than he is often given credit for when given a free hand, but had a pathological inability to cope with his political masters – a trait that would be just as apparent at Preston in 1648 as it was to be in 1645. Initially he outmanoeuvred Montrose and came very close to capturing him at Dundee, but on the battlefield he was more than a little unfortunate. He appears in fact to have been one of those generals who could bring his army advantageously to the battlefield but then had very little idea what to do with it once he'd got it there. Having been badly beaten at Alford he resigned his commission and thereafter served merely as a reluctant, and indeed downright obstructive, military advisor. Whilst his problems with political operators and appointees command a certain sympathy, perhaps his greatest failing, which again resurfaced at Preston, was a tendency to respond to them by abdicating any and all responsibility for anything.

Yet another professional soldier, this time from Pitfichie in Aberdeenshire, **Sir John Hurry** (sometimes erroneously referred to as Sir John Urry) had been the drillmaster of the Aberdeen Militia in the 1620s, but thereafter he mainly served as a cavalryman. Alongside Nathaniel Gordon, he initially served in the English Parliamentarian army at the outset of the Civil Wars, before defecting to the Royalists. Gordon returned to Scotland in order to follow his chief, the Marquis of Huntly, and afterwards Montrose. Hurry stayed for a time in England serving under Prince Rupert before once again changing sides at the end of 1644 and taking charge of Baillie's cavalry. In Scotland at least Hurry proved himself to be an excellent brigade commander and some of his minor operations, such as the raid on Aberdeen and the fighting retreat to Inverness, could well serve as practical illustrations of the precepts laid down in contemporary textbooks such as Cruso's *Militarie Instructions for the Cavallrie*. At Auldearn, however, in command of a comparatively large army of both infantry and cavalry, he would prove to be out of his depth.

OPPOSING ARMIES

The opposing Scots armies that fought in the Civil War enjoyed a considerable degree of commonality. Both were largely comprised of pikemen and musketeers (overwhelmingly equipped with matchlocks) levied out in traditional fashion by their feudal superiors either at the behest of the King's lieutenants or the Estates in Edinburgh. There were as a rule more Highland clansmen in the Royalist ranks than were levied out by the government, but it was rare for them to appear in appreciable numbers on either side. The popular image of Montrose leading an army of ferocious Highland warriors against a hapless band of Lowlanders served up for destruction in the name of the Covenant is a gross distortion of the actual, much more complex, picture.

THE ROYALISTS

The composition and character of the Royalist army was constantly evolving, but in broad terms it is possible to draw a fairly clear distinction between those troops who fought under Montrose during the first half of the campaign up to the winter battle of Inverlochy, and the army which fought at Auldearn and afterwards.

Prior to the fight at Inverlochy the greater part of the Royalist army was in fact made up of Irish mercenaries, originally recruited by Randal McDonnell, Earl of Antrim, and commanded in Scotland by a Hebridean exile named Alasdair MacColla. While formally organised in three regiments the brigade was, like most mercenary formations of the time, made up of individual companies of very diverse origins. Three of the companies were actually Hebridean Scots who formed MacColla's Lifeguard, but the remainder were indeed Irish, chiefly recruited in Ulster but including officers and men drawn from as far apart as Connaught and Dublin and even, according to John Spalding, some veterans of the famed Spanish Army of Flanders. If the bards are to be believed, some of the Hebrideans certainly had broadswords but the majority of the rank and file dressed in breeches and trews and were variously equipped with matchlock muskets and short pikes in the usual manner. These regulars accounted for most of the Royalist infantry at Tibbermore and at Aberdeen two weeks later. After this, however, like all 17th-century regiments they gradually and inevitably succumbed to exhaustion, disease and desertion. They still formed a significant part of the Royalist army at Inverlochy but thereafter their importance waned. This was exacerbated as MacColla became steadily more involved in rallying the Western clans for a private war against the clan Campbell. By 1645 the remaining mercenary companies appear to have been re-organised into just two small battalions commanded by colonels Laghtnan and O'Cahan.

The theory; a fully equipped musketeer as depicted by de Gehyn c.1603. Allowing for changes in fashion and the replacement of the large hat with a bonnet, most Scots regulars were kitted out as shown, although there is no evidence for the use of musket-rests.

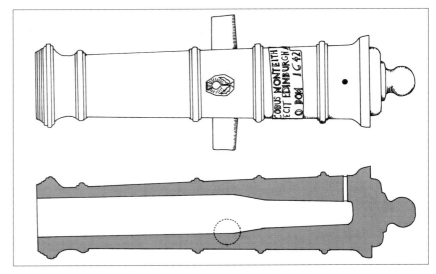

ABOVE **The reality; a Scots mercenary sketched by Köler in Stettin c.1631. The curious breeches may be intended to represent the normally close-fitting trews, but as equally close-fitting hose were still widely worn by German peasants it may be best to assume that the artist drew exactly what he saw.**

ABOVE, RIGHT **Artillery support for either side during the Civil War in Scotland was largely confined to light guns similar to this one cast in Edinburgh by James Monteith, although Baillie's army at Kilsyth had a larger piece named 'Prince Robert' which had originally been captured at Marston Moor.**

Happily for the Royalists, one of the principal results of the victory at Inverlochy on 2 February 1645 was the defection of a regular Covenanter cavalry regiment led by the Marquis of Huntly's eldest son, Lord Gordon. He was also able to levy substantial numbers of good infantry from amongst his father's people to replace the wastage amongst the Irish. At the same time he provided the Royalist army with the battle cavalry it needed to take on the veteran regiments being recalled from England. The quality of this cavalry was variable, ranging from Gordon's own regulars to so-called 'dragooners' who were literally no more than foot soldiers sitting on 'garrons' or very small ponies. Nevertheless cavalry formed an increasingly significant element of the Royalist army and its successes in 1645 sometimes owed more to this arm than to the vaunted Highlanders. Most were armed with swords and pistols, although there is evidence that some were lancers.

The Highland contingents marching with the Royalist army fell into three broad and overlapping categories. First there were the casual marauders who attached themselves in the expectation of plunder and usually melted away if there was any serious danger of fighting. Secondly there were various contingents drawn out of the Western Clans whose first priority was the war with the Campbells and who therefore marched with the army merely as allies, chiefly at Inverlochy and Kilsyth, but otherwise pursued their own objectives. The best of the Highlanders, however, were the regiments raised in Perthshire by Patrick Graham of Inchbrackie and in Upper Deeside by Donald Farquharson of Monaltrie. It is unlikely that they could ever be described as well disciplined, but they became good (and ultimately well-equipped) veteran soldiers. Monaltrie's men at least were described by one contemporary as a 'standing regiment' (i.e. regulars) and presumably included pikemen. Otherwise the clansmen who followed MacColla were pretty poorly armed. The men in the front rank generally had swords or axes, but those behind were only armed with dirks and bows. As a general rule of thumb, the smaller a Highland contingent the better armed.

Superficially, the Royalist army's tactical doctrine appears deceptively simple. A case can be made for reducing it to simply marching up close to

the enemy, firing a single volley and then launching a wild so-called 'Highland' charge. An argument has indeed been presented for crediting Alasdair MacColla with the 'invention' of these tactics, but in fact it was one commonly employed by many 17th-century armies – including the English Royalists at Naseby for one! However, as will become clear from the narrative, the battles were far more prolonged affairs than they might at first appear from the generally terse contemporary accounts. In fact the charge, far from being launched precipitately, was actually the culminating moment of a long and often inconclusive firefight. In the later battles it came more often than not after the Royalist cavalry had already moved against the flanks and rear of the enemy. Montrose's standard tactical repertoire was very largely restricted to holding fast in the centre until both opposing flanks had been driven or beaten in, and then launching at all-out attack to finish the affair.

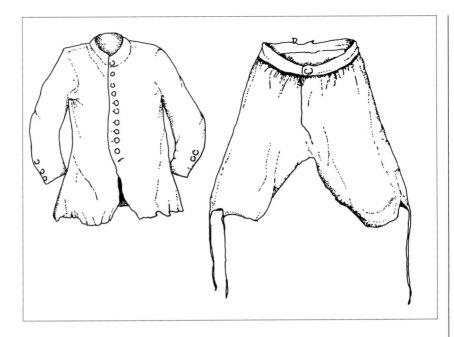

Coat and breeches recovered from a 17th-century corpse buried in a bog at Quintfall Hill in Sutherland. While coin evidence dated the presumed murder to the 1690s the style of the clothing – and particularly the stand-up collar – is much earlier. The buttons are balls of scrap cloth.

THE COVENANTERS

The Scots Army was a conscript force. In theory all those aged between the traditional ages of 16 and 60 were liable to turn out equipped with 'arms defencible' (hence their sometimes being designated 'fencibles') for up to 40 days' service at their own expense. If they were retained in service for longer, central government assumed responsibility for looking after them. In practice a series of preliminary musters whittled them down to a manageable pool of young and unmarried men who were actually fit for service, and even then it was customary to accept only one man in four or even just one in eight. Therefore, while a large number of troops were sent into England in 1644, a very substantial reserve of manpower remained behind that could be called out and formed into regiments either as reinforcements or for internal security duties. By and large it was these so-called 'second line' troops, occasionally boosted by burgh militias, who faced the veteran Irish mercenaries in the early stages of the campaign and this simple qualitative difference is alone sufficient to account for the Royalists' initial success. By 1645, however, not only did the survivors have a pretty good idea what they were doing, but the government had also recalled sufficient of its own veterans from England to take over from these levies. Consequently, although the Royalists continued to win battles, they faced a much harder job.

Few if any of the Scots infantry wore armour and they were generally equipped with either pikes or matchlock muskets, although towards the end of the war some men were kitted out with corselets and helmets and armed with halberds to take on Highland swordsmen. Ordinarily the cavalry similarly lacked armour although many had buff-coats and jacks. In general terms the cavalry relied upon their pistols and carbines rather than shock action, but significant numbers of them were armed with lances. Where possible it was customary to deploy regiments in two

squadrons; one comprising men armed with pistols and the other of lancers. Independent troops, of which there were a number, were normally armed with pistols rather than lances.

Artillery was occasionally used but generally in sieges rather than in the field. By and large the difficulty of transporting guns in a country that lacked good roads, and consequently relied upon pack animals for the movement of goods, meant that only the lightest and least effective pieces could be deployed.

OPPOSING PLANS

Highland bowman with helmet and mail shirt; this soldier's rather old-fashioned appearance indicates that he belongs to one of the western clans who fought under MacColla at Kilsyth.

A proper study of this important campaign is hampered by the quite dramatic imbalance in the available sources. During his later exile on the Continent Montrose's personal chaplain, George Wishart, wrote his famous *Memoirs of James, Marquis of Montrose*, a politically inspired hagiography that naturally presented his master's actions in the best possible light and employed considerable hindsight in explaining his decision-making. The central battle of this study, Auldearn, is traditionally represented as a carefully thought-out ambush in which Hurry was cunningly lured to his destruction. In reality it was a very confused, scrambling affair in which Hurry initially came perilously close to overrunning Montrose's cantonments before eventually being defeated in a seesaw battle that raged all day. Another result of the imbalance in the sources is that the dominant Royalist accounts set the agenda and the story becomes an account of their wanderings, punctuated by random encounters with an enemy displaying all the ineptness of a stage villain. Only thanks to the survival of a remarkable dossier of evidence, prepared by William Baillie for an inquiry into the debacle at Kilsyth, do we have anything like a proper account of the planning and decision-making on the other side. Useful as Ballie's dossier is, however, it is necessarily limited in its scope.

MONTROSE'S PLANS

It is still possible, however, to reconstruct in outline something of the basic planning on both sides. Montrose's primary objective was, quite clearly, to create enough havoc and diversion to force the recall of Leven's army from England. Ultimately he might even bring about a pro-Royalist counter-revolution in Scotland. He first needed to seize and hold a substantial area of territory long enough to recruit and sustain the forces necessary. He would, in the longer term, attempt to overthrow the government itself. Despite some quite appalling tactical defeats, the Scots government was initially able to prevent him from establishing this secure base. His celebrated marches were thus rather less daring adventures than harried efforts to keep one step ahead of his pursuers. The victory at Auldearn, however, although limited in its immediate scope, neutralised the northern army, giving him a free hand to seek out and destroy the Government's main field army under William Baillie.

THE COVENANTERS

The arrival of MacColla and his Irish mercenaries came as a salutary blow to the authorities in Edinburgh. Prior to the shocking disaster at

17

Tibbermore it had been sufficient to merely march an undisciplined rabble of more or less armed men into a disaffected area in the confident expectation that any dissidents would either flee or obligingly surrender themselves. The moveable goods of the dissidents were plundered to defray the costs of the punitive expedition and compensate both the officers and soldiers for their time and trouble. Now faced by an enemy that not only stood and fought back savagely but proved even more adept at plundering and wasting hostile territory, the Government's obvious remedy was to recall veteran units from England. This was of course exactly what Montrose and the King gambled on. Far from withdrawing Leven's army in its entirety, however, the Government held its nerve and settled for recalling substantial detachments from the larger regiments in the north of England and from Ulster. Military operations in England were not compromised. Once returned to Scotland, these troops were then for the most part formed into a field army whose sole purpose was to hunt down and destroy the rebels. The remaining local forces were henceforth to be used, so far as possible, in a defensive role, restricting the rebels' freedom of movement and above all denying them the opportunity to hold territory and attract recruits. The problem, however, was that while the field army was initially very successful in keeping the rebel army on the move, the local forces were too weak – and in some cases too unreliable – to pin the rebels down. They needed to be reinforced by units from the field army, which in turn reduced the latter's combat effectiveness.

The Brig o' Dee, Aberdeen. The scene of Montrose's victory over the Aberdeen Militia in 1639, while he was still serving the Covenant. Five years later he by-passed the bridge by crossing further upstream and approaching Aberdeen from the west.

THE CAMPAIGN BEGINS

Aberdeen: The Craibstane; an ancient boundary marker, it provides both the local name for Montrose's battle in 1644 – 'The Craibstane Rout' – and an earlier battle fought on the same spot in 1571.

On 27 June 1644 Alasdair MacColla finally sailed from Passage near Waterford in the south of Ireland with something short of 2,000 men. Landing at Ardnamurchan in the West Highlands, he first applied himself to the capture of Mingarry Castle to serve as a secure base and then marched eastwards in the hope of joining with the Marquis of Huntly. Unfortunately, as he had feared, it was already too late. Huntly, having disbanded his forces at the end of April, was in hiding in the far north of Scotland, and neither Sir James MacDonald of Sleat nor the Earl of Seaforth would call out their men to join the invaders. Eventually MacColla succeeded in virtually press-ganging about 500 men in Badenoch, but there was no disguising the fact that he was in trouble. He was in the classic predicament of a mercenary commander stranded in hostile territory without an employer for his hungry men. As forces began to assemble against him on all sides he turned south into Atholl where, seemingly by chance, he encountered the Marquis of Montrose at Blair. It is hard to be sure just how fortuitous this remarkable meeting actually was but, whether pre-arranged or accidental, the fact remained that Montrose was in need of an army and MacColla was just as desperately in need of an employer.

Happily conjoined and even reinforced by a small regiment raised in the area for Montrose by Patrick Graham of Inchbrackie, the two commanders then moved southwards towards the fair city of Perth. There on the morning of 1 September 1644 they found an army ranged against them on the broad expanse of Tibbermore.

TIBBERMORE

The Royalists afterwards claimed to have beaten upwards of 6,000 men but this estimate is absurdly high. Orders for Government troops to concentrate at Perth had only been issued four days earlier and at least some of the local levies, under Montrose's kinsman Lord Kilpont, had promptly joined the rebels instead. The Earl of Tullibardine had previously raised some 800 men at the time of Huntly's rising in April and, judging by the experience of other units, may still have had something above 600 in September. Another 800 had been ordered out of Dundee and Forfarshire, but it is uncertain whether they arrived in time, although 200 or so men can certainly be added from the Perth Militia. This would produce something between 1,600 and 2,400 infantry. There were also some levies from Fife, but in the circumstances it seems likely that all of them were included in the 400-odd cavalrymen under Lord Elcho and Sir James Scott of Rossie. The Government forces also had a couple of small cannon, but they proved largely ineffective.

Their dispositions were straightforward enough. Tullibardine commanded the infantry in the centre, Elcho had the cavalry on the right and Rossie had the cavalry on the left. Command of the whole was supposedly exercised by Lord Elcho despite the fact that he 'had no great character as a soldier', but in the event he confined himself to leading his cavalrymen.

Far from being heroically outnumbered, the Royalist army was in all probability larger than its opponents. In the centre alone most sources agree that Alasdair MacColla had something in the region of 2,000 men. About 1,500 of them were his seasoned Irish mercenaries, but he may also have had as many as 500 levies from Badenoch as well. All except the troops on the right and left wings were drawn up in six ranks. To reduce the chances of being outflanked by the Covenanters' cavalry, the troops on the wings deployed in only three ranks. The right wing, commanded by Montrose himself, consisted of Inchbrackie's Athollmen perhaps 500 strong, although this figure may be a little high. The left wing, commanded by Lord Kilpont, was similar in size and was made up of his own levies and some Keppoch MacDonalds. There were evidently some bowmen on this wing and on the slender evidence that Kilpont, like Montrose, had been a keen archer at university, many secondary sources identify all of his men as bowmen. In fact they are clearly described as being 'armed', i.e. properly equipped with musket and pike. The bowmen will actually have been the MacDonald clansmen.

All in all therefore the Royalists brought about 3,000 infantry on to the field against a Covenanter force of, at best, some 2,400 infantry and 400 cavalry. Moreover, whilst all of the Covenanters were raw levies, a substantial proportion of the Royalists were hardened veterans.

ORDER OF BATTLE
TIBBERMORE, 1 SEPTEMBER 1644

ROYALISTS

Perthshire levies (Graham of Inchbrackie)	500
Major Thomas Laghtnan's (Irish) Regiment	700
Colonel James McDonnell's (Irish) Regiment	400
Colonel Manus O'Cahan's (Irish) Regiment	400
Badenoch Levies	500
Perthshire Levies (Lord Kilpont)	500
MacDonalds of Keppoch	100

COVENANTERS

Regulars

Earl of Tullibardine's Regiment	600
Lord Elcho's Regiment	500

Levies

Dundee and Forfarshire	600
Perth Trained Bands	200

Cavalry

Sir James Scott of Rossie's Regiment }	
Lord Elcho's Regiment }	400

Aberdeen: This photograph, taken from the bottom of Clay Hill, gives a good impression of the strength of the position occupied by Burleigh's left wing – where the modern terrace of houses now stands.

As soon as the rebels came within cannon-shot, Tullibardine sent out a forlorn hope of musketeers under Lord Drummond. MacColla responded by sending out some skirmishers of his own who tumbled Drummond's men back in some confusion, whereupon Montrose ordered a general attack all along his line. The rebels, we are told quite specifically, had few long pikes (*hastis longioribus*) or even swords, which renders some of the more lurid popular accounts of hapless militiamen being literally cut down in an orgy of killing rather hard to justify. Instead, according to Patrick Gordon of Ruthven, the most objective of the chroniclers, they were 'at the first encounter with the Irishes played upon with hot alarums and continuall fyre'. In other words, in the centre there was a brief but decisive firefight in which the Irish prevailed over Tullibardine's 'ontryed men and fresh water shouldiours' and sent them running in panic-stricken flight.

On the Royalist right wing the battle was equally brief. The men of Atholl were not as well equipped as the Irish and a 1638 census carried out there had discovered only 100 out of 451 men armed with muskets. As MacColla led the centre forward against Tullibardine, Montrose led the Athollmen towards some comparatively high ground in time to face Rossie's cavalry and fire a single volley. This failed to stop the troopers and rather than waste time reloading, the Athollmen immediately came down the hill and 'with shoure of stones for want of more offensive armes, and lastly, with there swordes assailed both horse and foote men so desperately as they fell first in confusion and disordour'. The disorder increased when a specifically tasked detachment seized the cannon and turned them on their erstwhile owners.

By then it was pretty well all over. On the Royalist left neither Kilpont nor Elcho seem to have made any serious attempt to engage each other, although Ruthven suggests that the latter after falling back some distance 'strowe to rely and put themselves in better posture to renew the fight' only to be swept away by the fugitives. The pursuit was followed all the way into Perth and supposedly attended both by a considerable slaughter of the fugitives and a thorough plundering of the city. However, while the Royalists were obviously keen to emphasise the scale of their victory, and the Covenanters equally keen to trumpet the scale of the atrocity, the actual number of casualties may have been quite low. The Royalists can certainly have lost no more than a handful of men in the brief encounter and while more men are generally killed running away from battles than during the actual fighting, the fact that the Perth Militia had later to be physically restrained by their conquerors from setting their usual nightly watch suggests that their casualties had also been light.

As an immediate benefit the Royalists were able to replace clothing and re-equip themselves. With another army concentrating against them at Stirling, they headed eastwards to Dundee. The city was summoned to surrender on 6 September but answered defiantly and Montrose chose to head north to Aberdeen in the hope of raising Huntly's people.

THE CRAIBSTANE ROUT

Instead of Huntly, Montrose found another army thrown across his path just outside Aberdeen. All the available 'fencibles' from the Mearns, Aberdeenshire and Banffshire had been ordered to assemble at the burgh by 9 or 10 September, and the Morayshire Fencibles by 12 or 13 September. Unfortunately, with the Royalists moving north through their territory, the Mearns Fencibles refused to turn out. While the northern levies turned out, they failed to concentrate in time and only the local Aberdeenshire contingents had come in by the time Montrose arrived.

Nevertheless the Covenanter commander, Lord Balfour of Burleigh, was able to assemble two regiments of regulars – one he himself had

Aberdeen: The Royalist positions down in the valley of the How Burn as viewed from the dominant ridge line of Clay Hill.

brought from Fife commanded by Lieutenant-Colonel Charles Arnot and a newly raised Aberdeenshire regiment under Lord Forbes. These totalled something in the region of 900 men between them. In addition there was the Aberdeen Militia, 500 strong, all armed with muskets and commanded by a professional soldier, Major Arthur Forbes. There were also a number of smaller contingents from the surrounding areas under John Udny of Udny, James Hay of Muriefauld and John Keith of Clackbreach. It is unclear whether these fought as independent units or were brigaded in a single composite battalion. Burleigh may, therefore, have had as many as 1,900 or 2,000 foot. As at Perth, however, they were all largely untried. Ironically the most experienced unit was the part-time Aberdeen Militia, which had fought for the Royalists in 1639!

Burleigh also had at least three troops of regular cavalry, commanded by Captain Alexander Keith, Sir William Forbes of Craigievar and the youngest of Huntly's errant sons, Lord Lewis Gordon, besides some untrained fencibles under Lords Fraser and Crichton. This cavalry numbered about 300 in total.

On this occasion the Royalists were certainly outnumbered. After Tibbermore the Highlanders had returned to Badenoch, Atholl and Lochaber with their plunder. Kilpont's men had disbanded themselves after a now obscure dispute saw him murdered by his own second in command, Stewart of Ardvorlich. This left Montrose with little more than 1,500 infantry, almost all of them Irish and perhaps 60–80 cavalry – little more than moss-troopers – who came in under Nathaniel Gordon and Sir Thomas Ogilvy.

ORDER OF BATTLE
ABERDEEN, 13 SEPTEMBER 1644

ROYALISTS

Major Thomas Laghtnan's (Irish) Regiment	700
Colonel James McDonnell's (Irish) Regiment	400
Colonel Manus O'Cahan's (Irish) Regiment	400
MacDonalds of Keppoch	100
Nathaniel Gordon's Horse	40
Sir Thomas Ogilvy's Horse	40

COVENANTERS

Regulars

Lord Balfour of Burleigh's Regiment	500
Lord Forbes' Regiment	400

Levies

Aberdeen Militia (Major Arthur Forbes)	500
Aberdeenshire Fencibles	600

Cavalry

Sir William Forbes of Craigievar	50
Captain Alexander Keith	50
Lord Lewis Gordon	18
Lord Fraser	40
Lord Crichton	50
Abercrombie of Birkenbog	40
Arthur Forbes of Echt	40
John Forbes of Leslie	40

Conscious both of his own weakness and the strong position occupied by Burleigh's men on top of a steep ridge, Montrose opened proceedings by sending a formal summons to surrender. At Perth the messenger carrying his letter had been summarily tossed into jail, with the promise of a noose when the battle was over. At Aberdeen, however, the messenger was greeted courteously, offered light refreshments and sent back with a polite but firm refusal. Unfortunately, the effect was completely spoiled when on the way back the drummer accompanying the emissary was, quite wantonly, shot dead. If he had not already done so, Montrose at this point decided to storm the town and ordered his men to give no quarter.

The deployment of both armies was largely conventional. Burleigh's forces drew up along the crest of a flat-topped ridge about half a mile south of the burgh. The ridge was steepest at its western end where it overlooked a complex of buildings and ponds forming the Justice Mills. The Hardgate, the main road into the town from the south, crossed the How Burn about 100m downstream from the mills. The road went more or less straight up the face of the ridge and, although steep, the going was (and remains) easier than on the adjoining slope on either side. At the top it formed a Y junction, the main right fork carrying on into Aberdeen

while the left fork ran along the top of the ridge and then down to the mills. Eastwards from the Hardgate the ridge forms a steep crescent for another 150m or so but then becomes progressively lower.

Unsurprisingly, Burleigh placed most of his cavalry on this left flank while the three troops of regulars were posted on the right. The deployment of the infantry is somewhat more obscure, although it can largely be deduced from the course of events. The Fife Regiment was evidently on the left. This deployment makes sense as Burleigh considered it his best unit and this was the weakest part of his position. The Aberdeen Militia were probably in the centre alongside, if not actually astride, the

Aberdeen: Owing to a major error in scale Gardiner's faulty map of the battlefield represents all of Burleigh's forces crammed into the minor road junction depicted in this photograph.

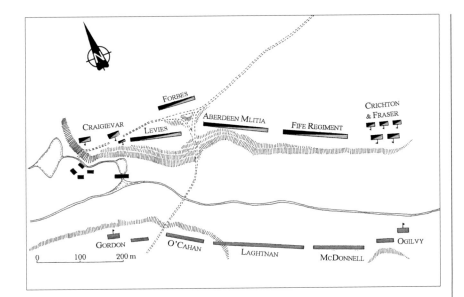

The true extent of the battlefield at the Justice Mills – otherwise known as the Craibstane Rout after an ancient marker stone at the road junction occupied by the northern levies.

Colonel's colour: Lord Balfour of Burleigh's Regiment. Although this striking all black colour was actually captured at Dunbar in 1650, the very prominent display of the maiden crest of Burleigh suggests that very similar colours may have been carried by the Fife Regiment, which he raised in 1644.

Hardgate. The fencibles under Udny and the others were on the right while Forbes' Regiment formed the reserve.

On the other side of the How Burn valley, Montrose must also have deployed most of his men to the east of the Hardgate. The rebel left, which was probably to the west of the road, was commanded by Colonel James Hay, a professional soldier who had been with Huntly in the spring. The rebel left wing included some 30 troopers under Nathaniel Gordon and 100 Irish musketeers commanded by Captain John Mortimer of O'Cahan's Regiment. The right wing, commanded by Sir William Rollo, consisted of Ogilvy's troopers and another 100 infantry. The infantry included some bowmen and therefore may have belonged to the Highland companies who usually acted as MacColla's lifeguard. MacColla himself was with Montrose in the centre, at the head of the three Irish regiments.

The battle began with an attempt by Hay's and Gordon's rebels to drive a detachment of Covenanter musketeers out of the Justice Mills. They succeeded in this but were immediately counter-attacked by Keith's cavalry troop. Gordon's moss troopers were outnumbered but a smart volley from Mortimer's musketeers sent Keith's men wheeling back in confusion, throwing away their lances as they went. Undaunted, Craigievar then advanced down the hill supported by Lord Forbes' Regiment from the reserve. Unfortunately, instead of driving forward and rolling up the Royalists' left flank, Forbes' men contented themselves with establishing a strong defensive position in the upper mills. A firefight immediately developed with Mortimer's men in the lower mill but, when Nathaniel Gordon fetched some rebel reinforcements, Craigievar led his cavalry out against O'Cahan's Regiment.

First Lord Lewis Gordon with his 18 troopers trotted up and fired their pistols. This was largely ineffective, although it is hard to see what else they might have done in the circumstances. They did however succeed in drawing the fire of O'Cahan's Regiment. This was probably exactly what they intended for the Irish were then charged by Craigievar's own troop. Notwithstanding, the Irish mercenaries 'being so well trained men as the

world could afford no better', opened their intervals to let the cavalry ride through, before turning and firing a volley into their backs. As the Covenanter horse stumbled in disorder Nathaniel Gordon's Royalist horse charged and routed them, capturing both Craigievar and his second in command Forbes of Boyndlie.

It was a similar story on the Royalist right wing where Lords Fraser and Crichton twice led their rabble of horsemen down against Sir William Rollo and McDonnell's Irish Regiment. Neither attack was pressed home with much resolution, although Sir Thomas Ogilvy had his horse shot from under him and Ogilvy of Inverquharity suffered a lance thrust in the thigh. These actions did, nevertheless, prevent both O'Cahan's and McDonnell's regiments taking part in the main rebel assault on Burleigh's centre. Recognising there was no alternative, Montrose ordered Laghtnan's Regiment to 'lay aside their Muskets and Pikes, and fall on with Sword and Durk.'

It is unlikely that the assault was quite so precipitate as this suggests for the slope is extremely steep and according to Ruthven the fight 'was disputed hard for a long space'. Instead, as at Tibbermore, the decisive charge was launched as the culmination of the firefight. Either way it was devastatingly effective, for the Aberdeen Militia immediately gave way and fled back towards the town. Naturally enough Laghtnan's men went after them, chasing them back into the streets and killing, according to the meticulous John Spalding, 118 of them. With O'Cahan's men still held up down by the Justice Mills, Forbes' Regiment and the northern levies under Udny escaped virtually unscathed, but the Fife Regiment was less fortunate. Amidst the rout they 'lyk bold and well trained souldiours' held together and began marching off to the east in the hope of working around the rebels' flank and getting over the nearby river. Instead MacColla 'takes furth four hundreth Irishes' – presumably McDonnell's Regiment – and scattered them with considerable loss of life.

The most precise accounting puts Burleigh's losses at 520 and nearly all the accounts agree that apart from the Aberdeen men most of the dead belonged to the Fife Regiment. Royalist casualties were clearly much lighter but the four days of rape and pillage that followed did far more damage to the Royalist cause than Burleigh's muskets.

From Aberdeen the rebels straggled out to Kintore laden with plunder that, in MacColla's own words, 'hath made all our soldiers cavaliers'. On 16 September they then retreated westwards into the wild fastness of Rothiemurchus.

The Marquis of Argyle was just three days behind them and leading a substantial force including three regiments of Highlanders from Argyllshire and, stiffening these rather unreliable levies, two good regiments (the Earl of Lothian's and Sir Mungo Campbell of Lawers') from Ireland – some 4,000 infantry in all. He also had the Earl of Dalhousie's regular cavalry, which had lately fought at Marston Moor, and ten other troops of horse perhaps numbering as many as 900 troopers in all. Craigievar's troop was detached shortly afterwards but replaced by a third regiment of regular infantry under the Laird of Buchanan.

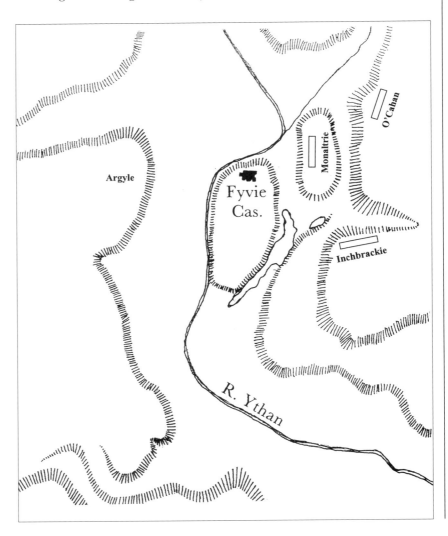

The battlefield at Fyvie 1644; Royalist dispositions are reconstructed but it is impossible to establish Argyle's dispositions with any certainty.

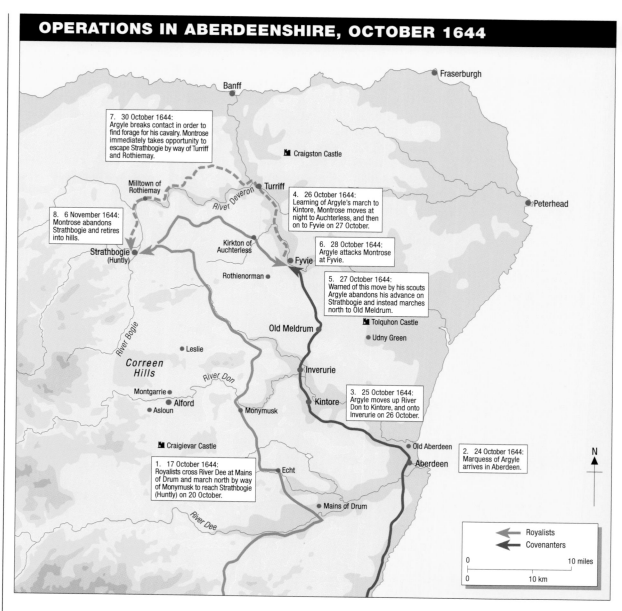

7. 30 October 1644:
Argyle breaks contact in order to find forage for his cavalry. Montrose immediately takes opportunity to escape Strathbogie by way of Turriff and Rothiemay.

8. 6 November 1644:
Montrose abandons Strathbogie and retires into hills.

4. 26 October 1644:
Learning of Argyle's march to Kintore, Montrose moves at night to Auchterless, and then on to Fyvie on 27 October.

6. 28 October 1644:
Argyle attacks Montrose at Fyvie.

5. 27 October 1644:
Warned of this move by his scouts Argyle abandons his advance on Strathbogie and instead marches north to Old Meldrum.

3. 25 October 1644:
Argyle moves up River Don to Kintore, and onto Inverurie on 26 October.

2. 24 October 1644:
Marquess of Argyle arrives in Aberdeen.

1. 17 October 1644:
Royalists cross River Dee at Mains of Drum and march north by way of Monymusk to reach Strathbogie (Huntly) on 20 October.

Royalists
Covenanters

In the face of this threat the Royalists quite literally commenced marching in circles. While Argyle moved west they found their way into Moray blocked on Speyside by another regular cavalry regiment commanded by Lord Gordon, the Marquis of Huntly's errant son, and instead turned southwards into Atholl. Doggedly following in their tracks Argyle was at Ruthven in Badenoch when he heard that they had split up. MacColla had insisted on taking 500 of his men off to the West Highlands, ostensibly to relieve his garrisons there. Argyle thereupon took the opportunity to split his own forces, throwing a strong garrison (Lawers' and Buchanan's regiments) into Inverness and arranging for its fortification before setting off in pursuit once more. Montrose thereupon swung south past Perth and then north again, back towards Aberdeen. This time a regular officer, Sir James Ramsay, blocked their

Fyvie Castle, Aberdeenshire, the scene of Montrose's defensive action against Argyle.

path at the Brig o' Dee, forcing them to cross further upstream by the Mills of Drum and then march north to Strathbogie.

There he tried to raise the Gordons but was greatly hampered, not only by Huntly's continued absence, but also by the fact that Lord Gordon was still operating in the area. Nevertheless he still managed to pick up 200 good infantry from the old Strathbogie Regiment and another 200 Highlanders under Farquharson of Monaltrie, and perhaps another 100 from Strathavan. In addition he still had about 800 Irish mercenaries and 200 of Inchbrackie's men, making about 1,500 in all. This was just as well as Argyle reached Aberdeen on 24 October and set off in pursuit again the next day with 2,000 foot and a considerable body of cavalry.

At this point an intelligence failure nearly resulted in disaster for the Royalists. Learning that Argyle was in the vicinity of Aberdeen, Montrose moved eastwards to Auchterless on the night of 25 October and from there to Fyvie the next day. Presumably some cunning plan was afoot but it unravelled at once when Argyle learned of this move and attacked him there on 28 October.

Fyvie

Ruthven helpfully states that the rebels had the river Ythan on their right and a wood on their left, with what he describes as a 'hollow bruick' to their front, which implies that they were facing southwards. However, as Argyle's cavalry was quartered around Rothienorman and Auchterless, to the west of Fyvie, it would seem that this initial position was soon abandoned in favour of a westward-facing one on the high ground overlooking the castle. Even so Montrose was still able to make use of the 'hollow bruick', which was evidently the stream that emerges from a prominent re-entrant in the hillside about 300 metres south of the castle. Immediately to the north of this stream, and between the castle and the hillside, is a low rise that creates an area of dead ground at the foot of the hill. Both this rise and the adjacent hillside were divided up by turf walls, which gave them an 'appearance like a camp'. Indeed, their remains are sometimes said to be trenches dug by the Royalists, although they were actually agricultural in origin.

The constricted and partially wooded nature of the ground meant that the fighting never developed into a general engagement. This was

FOR
RELIGION

Covenant   And

The
Cuntrie

These colours – a white saltire on blue – were carried by the Earl of Kinghorn's men in 1639 and may also have been carried by his tenants who fought at Aberdeen under the Laird of Udny in 1644.

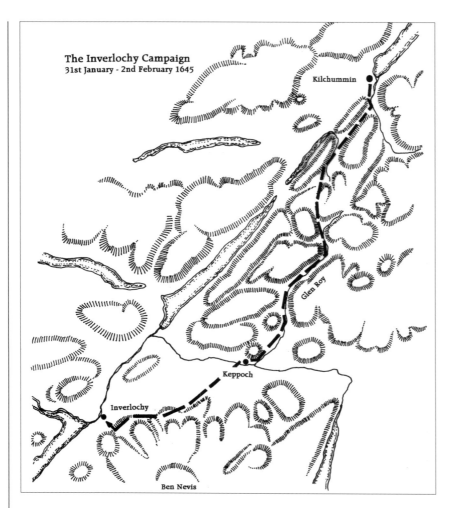

Kilchummin

Glen Roy

Keppoch

Inverlochy

Ben Nevis

The Inverlochy campaign saw Montrose and MacColla undertake an extremely bold march over the mountains flanking the Great Glen in order to launch a surprise attack on the Marquis of Argyle's army at Inverlochy on Candlemas Day.

perhaps just as well for the rebels since the Strathbogie men deserted en masse at the very outset. Perhaps encouraged by this, Lothian's regulars attacked and carried the enclosures at the bottom of the hill, although an immediate Royalist counter-attack, probably by Monaltrie's men, retook them without much of a fight.

Argyle's riposte was to send forward five troops of cavalry. This time the Royalists abandoned the position without a fight, but only to lure the horsemen into a trap. Unfortunately, the trap was sprung too soon when Inchbrackie's Athollmen fired from the cover of the woods. The cavalry immediately halted and started to pull back, whereupon the rebel infantry emerged from the trees and rushed forward with a loud shout, only to be attacked in turn by Captain Alexander Keith's troop. Although he himself was killed, the charge succeeded in covering the retreat of the other four troops but was unable to prevent the rebels from re-occupying the enclosures. Another attack by both infantry and cavalry was made sometime during the afternoon but never seems to have properly got under way. Argyle was reluctant to employ his raw and poorly armed Highland levies and without them considered his infantry too weak to carry the position.

Desultory skirmishing continued for another two days before a shortage of fodder for his cavalry forced Argyle to pull back some two miles to Crichie. A greatly relieved Montrose promptly decamped in the opposite direction, first to Turriff and then west into Badenoch and so back to Atholl. Argyle pursued him as far as Strathbogie but the rebel army was melting away. Even Nathaniel Gordon changed sides again on 3 November, bringing in Forbes of Craigievar by way of insurance. Argyle returned to Edinburgh, confident that the onset of winter would be sufficient to finish the Royalist rebels off.

THE WINTER OF 1644–45

Far from snuffing out the rebellion, the winter instead saw it unexpectedly flare up again. At the end of November MacColla rejoined Montrose at Blair Atholl, bringing not only his Irish troops but perhaps as many as 1,000 of the Western clans as well. However, he also brought his own agenda. Montrose had been intending to winter in the Lowlands, presumably in Strathbogie. MacColla, however, insisted that their combined forces instead launch a midwinter raid on Inverary, the long-secure seat of Clan Campbell. Unusually mild weather left the mountain passes open and by 13 December, having met no resistance, they were laying waste to Argyllshire. Although the castle itself held out, Inverary town was captured and Argyle himself forced to flee in his galley.

Safely back in the Lowlands, Argyle unsurprisingly set about co-ordinating an immediate counter-attack and Lieutenant-General William Baillie, who had just been recalled from England, was ordered to march his regulars westward on 20 December. However, at Gairlochhead he met with Argyle and had the first of what was to be a series of disagreements. Argyle wanted him to march into the Highlands, but

A reconstruction by English Civil War Society members carrying both Royalist and Covenanting colours retraces the path followed by Montrose's army down Glen Roy on the march to Inverlochy.

A Highland chieftain by MacIan; although notionally identified as a MacLean, this style of dress would be more likely to be found east of the Great Glen.

Baillie, not unreasonably, pointed out that it would be extremely difficult to support the army there in the winter. It was eventually agreed that instead Baillie should base himself at Perth with the bulk of his forces while Argyle pursued the rebels, who were by then moving northwards into Lorne and Lochaber.

As usual they were also haemorrhaging men and when Montrose halted at Kilchummin (modern Fort Augustus) on 31 January he had less than 2,000 with him. There he also learned that a considerable body of Northern Levies under the Earl of Seaforth had reinforced the Inverness garrison ahead of him while Argyle was closing in behind him at Inverlochy. Both ends of the Great Glen were therefore blocked. Although there was nothing to prevent the Royalists from marching up Glen Tarf and across the Corrieyairack Pass into Speyside, Montrose took the bold decision to double back and attack Argyle.

Knowing a straightforward advance would be detected almost immediately, the rebels first marched due south up Glen Tarff as far as Culachy and then moved parallel to the Great Glen as far as Glen Buck, shielded by the long ridges of Meall a Cholumain and Druim Laragan. Thus far the going was relatively easy, but then they had to cross the gorge of the Calder Burn to reach the head of the glen. At that point they were about 1,000 feet above sea-level and then had another 1,000 feet to climb to reach the col at Carn na Larach. Passing on to the windswept Teanga plateau, they then faced a steep descent into Glen Turret. Although many weary miles remained in front of them after that, the worst was over and they made good time down Glen Turret and then Glen Roy to Keppoch. There the Royalist advance guard evicted one of Argyle's outposts and rested for three hours in a barn (still standing today) while the rest of the army caught up.

Setting off again they then forded the river Spean at Corriechoille and pushed on through the Leanachan Woods by moonlight and finally threw themselves down, exhausted, at Torlundy overlooking Inverlochy. It was the early hours of 2 February 1645, Candlemas Day, and in just 36 hours they had marched as many miles through the hills in midwinter and were now poised to fight an army twice their size.

Inverlochy

The Royalists had only about 1,500 men divided into four 'divisions'. Alasdair MacColla took command of the right at the head of Laghtnan's Irish Regiment, which was still about 400 strong. In the centre were about 500 Highlanders largely drawn from the Western Clans – MacDonalds, MacLeans and Appin Stewarts – and probably some of Inchbrackie's Athollmen as well. The left wing was formed by Colonel Manus O'Cahan's Irish Regiment and, in reserve behind the centre, was the third Irish regiment, McDonnell's and some more Highlanders. It is possible the latter may have been Inchbrackie's men, but in the circumstances it is more likely that they were an ad hoc formation made up of those clansmen too exhausted to stand in the front line. Nearby was a small troop of about 50 cavalry under Sir Thomas Ogilvy.

Below them the Covenanters adopted similar dispositions. Argyle prudently retired to his galley, moored offshore, and turned command of the army over to an experienced soldier, Sir Duncan Campbell of Auchinbrec. According to Gordon of Ruthven, there was a strong body of Highlanders, armed with guns, bows and axes, posted a little way in front of the main body. This was presumably Argyle's own regiment recalled from Ireland, for the description clearly implies that the clansmen standing behind them were more poorly armed levies. There seems to have been about 1,500 infantry in the centre in total. The wings of the army comprised 16 companies of regulars borrowed from Baillie's army and formed into two provisional battalions under Lieutenant-Colonel Lachlan Roughe of the Earl of Tullibardine's Regiment and Lieutenant-Colonel John Cockburn of the Earl of Moray's Regiment. Set back a little from the main body, two light cannon were deployed on a slight eminence and the left wing of the army was anchored on the ruined Inverlochy Castle, itself garrisoned by 50 musketeers.

ORDER OF BATTLE
INVERLOCHY, 2 FEBRUARY 1645

ROYALISTS

Colonel Thomas Laghtnan's Regiment	400
Colonel Manus O'Cahan's Regiment	200
Colonel James McDonnell's Regiment	200
Western Clans	500 (approx.)
Patrick Graham of Inchbrackie's Regiment	200
Sir Thomas Ogilvy's Horse	50

COVENANTERS

Marquis of Argyle's Regiment	500
Campbell levies	1000

'Commanded companies'

Lieutenant-Colonel Lachlan Roughe's Battalion	200
Lieutenant-Colonel John Cockburn's Battalion	200

Having spent a cold and hungry night the rebels had no reason to stand around and at dawn they immediately rolled down the hillside. For some reason the Irish advanced more briskly than the Highlanders in the centre and so came into contact first. As they closed they came under fire from Roughe and Cockburn's men, but held their own fire until the very last moment when they fired a single crashing volley into the regulars that 'fyred there beards' and followed it up with a charge with swords and pikes. Not surprisingly the Covenanters broke and ran.

In the centre Montrose met with even less resistance. Argyle's Regiment fired a single volley at long range and then broke and ran as the rebel Highlanders came running up, falling back on the levies behind who were infected by the same panic. There was very little fighting as such but rather a ruthless massacre perpetrated by one set of feuding clansmen upon another.

Debacle at Dundee
The victory at Inverlochy brought in substantial numbers of recruits for the first time; more than enough to compensate for those who had

Clansman with two-handed sword; these weapons were little mentioned in inventories or literary sources by the middle of the 17th century. The clubbed hair appears at first sight to be anachronistic, but not only was it highly practical but excavations in Aberdeen's Gallowgate uncovered a number of casualties from Huntly's battle in 1646 – all of them with their hair clubbed in this way.

drifted away during the winter or been lost in the fighting or afterwards. Some were of course merely making their peace with what was, for the moment, the winning side. On 19 February, however, Lord Gordon defected to the rebels at the head of his regular cavalry regiment, delivered up the city of Elgin, which he had been charged with defending, and thereafter devoted himself to raising his father's people for the King's service.

By the latter part of March, Montrose was able to move southwards from Aberdeen with about 3,000 infantry. Rather less than a third of them were Irish by this time and the only Highlanders were the small regiments commanded by Graham of Inchbrackie and Farquharson of Monaltrie. Fully half of the infantry were Lowland Scots including the Strathbogie Regiment, which was to earn itself something of a reputation in the coming months. Montrose was also able to field an effective force of cavalry for the first time. Some of the 300 troopers were survivors of Ogilvie's faithful little troop. Significantly, of the others most were not the rude multitude of 'bonnet lairds on cart-horses' imagined by popular historians, but Gordon's regulars – and it would show.

In the meantime the Government was also gathering its forces under Lieutenant-General William Baillie. His cavalry commander, Sir John Hurry, was proving uncomfortably aggressive. In a classic operation on the evening of 15 March he had beaten up Royalist quarters in Aberdeen, killing one of Montrose's more promising officers, young Farquharson of Monaltrie, whose regiment then went to James Farquharson of Inverey. Hurry in turn appeared to get the worst of a skirmish at Halkerton Wood near Fettercairn a week later. But he was able to alert Baillie to the fact that, as soon as the rebel army crossed the river Dee, its Aberdeenshire levies began drifting away in appreciable numbers. Bolstered by this happy news Baillie took up a strong position at Ruthven on the river Isla. Montrose duly approached, declined to force a crossing and then after some shuffling retreated into the hills and occupied Dunkeld. There even more of the levies took the opportunity to slip off home and Montrose realised he had to do something positive before the army disintegrated completely.

Misled by a false report that Baillie had crossed the river Tay at Perth, Montrose decided to mount a daring raid on the city of Dundee. Sending all but 300 of the Irish up to Blair Atholl with the baggage train, he marched eastwards to Blairgowrie with the rest of his forces on the night of 3 April. There he picked out 600 musketeers and the 200 troopers of Lord Gordon's Horse and, sending the others northwards to Brechin, made straight for Dundee where he arrived shortly before dawn.

Instead of attacking at once however the rebels rested up for some hours and a Lieutenant John Gordon afterwards told his interrogators that he was roused at 10.00am to take in a summons. However, the burgh's militia were under the command of a Lieutenant-Colonel Cockburn, who had been captured and paroled at Inverlochy, and had no intention of repeating the experience. How long the formalities lasted is unclear but to Gordon's dismay the attack began before he was able to return with a reply and he was promptly flung into jail where he remained throughout what followed.

Royalist accounts suggest that the town was stormed in very short order and that while the militia did indeed make a fight of it Montrose and the Irish quickly broke in by the West Port or gate, while Lord Gordon forced the North Port. On the other hand it is equally clear from what happened next that it was late in the afternoon before the city was properly in rebel hands.

Unfortunately, just as they reached the market place and began dispersing in the customary orgy of plundering, word came that Baillie, far from sitting quietly unawares at Perth, was only two miles away and coming on fast! Needless to say this news produced absolute pandemonium. The bacchanalia was interrupted before it had gotten properly under way and, according to legend, the rebel rearguard tumbled out through the East Port just as Baillie stormed in by the West – leaving poor Lieutenant Gordon still locked up in the tollbooth! Happily Baillie and his men were themselves exhausted by their forced march from Perth and, in a desperate attempt to save the town, he had left his infantry behind on the road. Consequently he now took the unfortunate, but understandable, decision to wait for them before embarking on a pursuit of the rebels.

By the time he got his men on the march again darkness had fallen. Hurry, commanding the cavalry, soon caught up with the rebel rearguard, which was still only a few miles east of the town. There was a brief fight but in the dark Hurry was unwilling to press forward without infantry support and allowed the rebels to break contact once again. Taking advantage of this respite, the rebels turned northwards at midnight off the main road at Muirdrum while Hurry, unaware, pressed on to Arbroath. Only there did he realise what had happened, but instead of wasting time by retracing his steps he turned north and succeeded in throwing his men across the Brechin road at Froickheim. This forced Montrose and his weary men to veer aside to Guthrie and for a time there was a danger that they might be caught between Hurry's cavalry and Baillie's infantry marching up the road to Forfar. Indeed Baillie was at Forfar by dawn but, despite repeated orders to attack, Hurry had been content to maintain his position during the night instead of trying to force the rebels further westwards. Consequently they managed to get across the South Esk at Careston. With the daylight Hurry got on their track again but by then it was too late and, after a last

One of a number of colours carried by Irish mercenaries embarked for Scotland in 1644. All had a yellow canton with a red cross and an imperial crown beneath. This particular one was white with a 'blood red' crucifix on it.

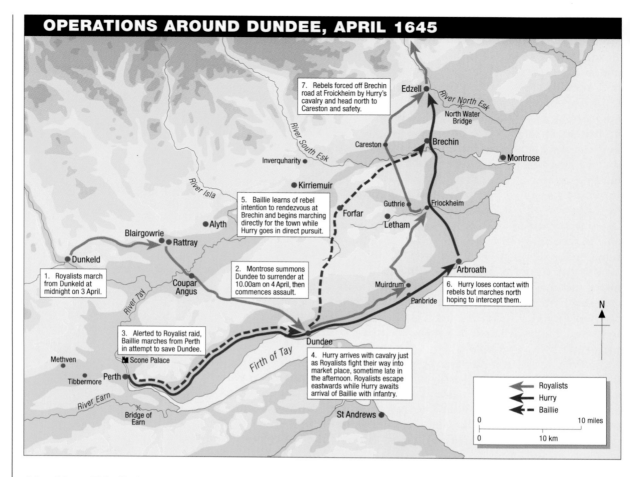

7. Rebels forced off Brechin road at Froickheim by Hurry's cavalry and head north to Careston and safety.

5. Baillie learns of rebel intention to rendezvous at Brechin and begins marching directly for the town while Hurry goes in direct pursuit.

1. Royalists march from Dunkeld at midnight on 3 April.

2. Montrose summons Dundee to surrender at 10.00am on 4 April, then commences assault.

6. Hurry loses contact with rebels but marches north hoping to intercept them.

3. Alerted to Royalist raid, Baillie marches from Perth in attempt to save Dundee.

4. Hurry arrives with cavalry just as Royalists fight their way into market place, sometime late in the afternoon. Royalists escape eastwards while Hurry awaits arrival of Baillie with infantry.

Royalists / Hurry / Baillie

skirmish at Edzell, he let them go and fell back to rejoin a thoroughly exasperated Baillie at Brechin.

The march to Auldearn

Having abandoned their pursuit of the rebels Hurry and Baillie parted company in ill humour. A deputation from Aberdeenshire turned up at Brechin on 5 April and pressed for the urgent assistance of some regulars to counter the growing threat posed there by the Gordons. Baillie reluctantly agreed to send Hurry with some 160 cavalry drawn from Sir James Halkett's Regiment and two veteran infantry units – the Lord Chancellor's Regiment and the long-suffering Earl of Lothian's Regiment.

Baillie then returned to Perth with the rest of his army. On 17 April he attacked Montrose's cantonments at Crieff. Both Lord Gordon and Alasdair MacColla were away now, leaving Montrose with just a couple of hundred infantry and a handful of cavalry, so another undignified flight followed up into Strathearn. However, Montrose then doubled back, by-passed Baillie and pushed south as far as Doune Castle not far to the north of Stirling. There on 20 April he rendezvoused with Lord Gordon's younger brother, Viscount Aboyne, who until then had been in the Royalist garrison of Carlisle. Montrose also took the opportunity to get a dispatch away to the King.

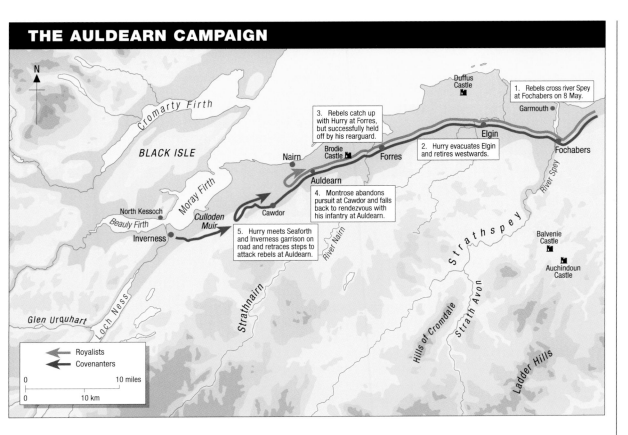

1. Rebels cross river Spey at Fochabers on 8 May.

2. Hurry evacuates Elgin and retires westwards.

3. Rebels catch up with Hurry at Forres, but successfully held off by his rearguard.

4. Montrose abandons pursuit at Cawdor and falls back to rendezvous with his infantry at Auldearn.

5. Hurry meets Seaforth and Inverness garrison on road and retraces steps to attack rebels at Auldearn.

Royalists
Covenanters

0   10 miles
0   10 km

Having picked up Aboyne, Montrose then hurried north again to meet with Lord Gordon and Alasdair MacColla on Deeside. The arrival of Hurry's regulars was threatening the Royalists' nascent power-base in the north-east of Scotland. Although delayed by a mutiny amongst his unpaid soldiers, Hurry had left Aberdeen on 17 April and embarked on a broad sweep towards Inverness, where he sent orders for the Earls of Seaforth and Sutherland to assemble their levies. On the way he also picked up Lord Findlater's newly raised regiment and recruited a number of dragooners, together with other levies, all of them eager to avenge the rebel depredations.

In the face of this advance Lord Gordon prudently suspended his own recruiting and retired into the hills by way of Auchindoun. Once all three elements of the Royalist army had re-united, they agreed their first priority had to be the destruction of Hurry's army – an entirely predictable response that suited Hurry's plans perfectly. He crossed over the river Spey on 3 May and at a meeting, probably in Elgin, with Seaforth and the Laird of Innes, representing the northerners and the government's local supporters respectively, it was resolved to turn and fight as soon as all three contingents could be concentrated. In the meantime the last thing Hurry wanted to do was to scare off the rebels before the Covenanter concentration was complete and so he lingered at Elgin until the rebels too crossed the Spey, either late on 7 May or more likely 8 May. Hurry then retired very slowly through Forres.

Hurry may not have been an outstanding military commander but he was a very competent professional soldier and his fighting retreat was a textbook operation. Covered by his cavalry, his infantry steadily fell back in two- or three-mile bounds, halting repeatedly to cover the cavalry as they in turn fell back, then repeating the process. For the Royalists it was a slow and frustrating business. Hurry held the initiative throughout the day and, while losing 15 or 16 troopers, seemingly took no casualties amongst his infantry. Montrose's losses are largely unknown but were clearly sufficient to keep him at a respectful distance. One casualty who can be identified, however, was young James Gordon of Rhynie; wounded during the crossing of the Spey and subsequently murdered in his bed by some of the Laird of Innes' men. This pointless killing only led to reprisals by Lord Gordon's men in the coming battle.

Montrose's own account has in the past been interpreted to mean that he actually pursued Hurry all the way to Inverness on 7 May, retired back to the village of Auldearn just outside Nairn on 8 May and was attacked there by Hurry on the morning of 9 May. This seems rather unlikely. Montrose himself actually claimed that his running fight with Hurry's rearguard covered 14 miles, while one of his men, Patrick Gordon of Ruthven, wrote afterwards that the first clash occurred at Forres. Assuming both are correct, and there is no reason to doubt it, this would suggest that Montrose followed Hurry no further than Cawdor, while Ruthven clearly states that the rebels actually halted at Auldearn. The obvious inference is that after that first action at Forres, Montrose and the cavalry pushed on as far as Cawdor, before falling back again to rendezvous with the slower-moving infantry in Auldearn at, or shortly after, nightfall. Montrose had, unwittingly, broken contact with Hurry just as the latter was about to receive significant reinforcement.

THE BATTLE OF AULDEARN

On the night of 8 May the Royalist rebels were quartered in and around the small village of Auldearn. From the evidence of subsequent events it would seem that the village itself was only occupied by the Highlanders of Alasdair MacColla's Lifeguard and one of Lord Gordon's units – William Gordon of Monymore's newly raised regiment from Strathavan. The rest of the army was scattered somewhat to the east of it. John Spalding's account blandly, but rather tellingly, states that they camped 'commodiously', which suggests that with the weather coming on to rain they spread themselves far around the countryside, seeking shelter in cottages and barns over a very broad area. At any rate after the battle began next morning it certainly appears to have taken some hours to concentrate them again.

When the Royalists last saw Hurry's army, at dusk on the previous day, it had still been marching away from them down the road to Inverness. This had generated a false sense of security amongst the Royalists, one symptom of which was this wide dispersal of troops. The other result was a near-fatal failure to maintain contact. As Patrick Gordon of Ruthven later commented; 'Above all things they should have been carefull of intelligence, either by disguysed espyels, as some choose subtill and darring men in beggeres weid or womenes apparell, or a pairtie send forth to catch ane centrie or bring in a prisoner; for want of which intelligence, if God had not prevented it beyond all expectation all ther throats had bein cutt.'

Auldearn: This view of Garlic Hill from the base of the castle hill gives a good idea of how it is the dominant feature of the central part of the battlefield. Hurry's army attacked from right to left along the top of it.

Instead, Montrose merely contented himself with setting a strong 'watch' or picquet, together with sentries 'on all quarters'. The sentries were, however, poorly supervised in what turned out to be a dark night of pouring rain and by morning all seem to have crammed themselves into Auldearn village with Monymore's Strathavan men. Consequently, shortly before dawn Alasdair MacColla rousted out half a dozen of them 'as God would have it' and ordered them to scout down the road at first light. It is easy enough to guess what they thought of their assignment but, as Ruthven remarked, they saved the rebels from having their throats cut, for borne on the wind they heard a 'thundring report' as hundreds of men cleared their muskets.

Somewhere to the west of Cawdor, Hurry had rendezvoused in the dark with the Inverness garrison and Seaforth's northern levies. About-facing immediately, he marched hard back up the road, hoping to surprise the rebels in their beds and destroy them in detail before they could concentrate. He might well have succeeded had he not halted about four miles short of his objective to let his men clear and reload their muskets before launching their assault. This may have been a good idea but, rather than waiting while the old charges were drawn, Hurry simply left the road, turned down towards the sea and had the men fire off their muskets. MacColla's scouts, warned by the noise of the volley, quickly ran back to rouse the sleeping soldiers in the village while Nathaniel Gordon, who had once again changed sides in February, sought out Montrose to warn him that they were about to be attacked.

THE ARMIES

Hurry by now had no fewer than five regiments of regular infantry under his command. These included his original two – Lothian's and the Lord Chancellor's – the Earl of Findlater's, which he had picked up

TOP **Auldearn: Kinnudie as seen by Alasdair MacColla's forces on top of Garlic Hill at the outset of the battle. Hurry's original position is marked by the line of trees in the middle distance.**

ABOVE **This colour carried by an Irish mercenary company was the only one with a yellow field and was almost certainly the one carried by MacColla's men at Auldearn. The motto – 'may God arise and his enemies be scattered' is certainly appropriate.**

Auldearn: The village as seen from Hurry's later command post on top of Garlic Hill. From here the strength of the Royalist position is not immediately apparent. The castle hill is marked by the lone white building on the left (Boath Doocot) and the church appears to be in the centre.

on the road, and two more from the Inverness garrison; Sir Mungo Campbell of Lawers' and the Laird of Buchanan's. The victorious Royalists afterwards crowed that all five were well trained and indeed the best troops in the kingdom. This was true only up to a point; Lawers', Lothian's and the Lord Chancellor's regiments were certainly veterans but Buchanan's, although raised in 1644, had never seen action. The Earl of Findlater's had only been commissioned at the beginning of March 1645. If each of these regiments mustered an average of 500 men, Hurry would have had 2,500 regulars at his disposal. However, this is almost certainly far too high and 400 men each is probably nearer the mark for the three 'old' regiments. Buchanan's on the other hand provided only a detachment, probably no more than 200 strong, since the greater part of the regiment was left guarding Inverness. Recruiting in a disputed area, it is impossible to say how successful the Earl of Findlater had been. In the circumstances he will probably have been lucky to bring more than 300 men to Auldearn.

Besides these 1,700 or so regulars, Hurry also had two newly raised regiments brought in by the Earls of Seaforth and Sutherland. Seaforth still had some 300 men (armed with pike and musket) in July so, allowing for casualties and deserters, he may well have mustered around 500 in May. Sutherland brought about the same from Strathnavar. In addition there were also several hundred hastily assembled local levies including the Laird of Grant's men and the Frasers from Beuly. All in all therefore Hurry must have had something in the region of 3,000 infantry of variable quality.

Hurry's cavalry are less easy to reconstruct. Some chroniclers estimate he may have had as many as 600 or 700 but this is certainly too high. The best of them were the 160 troopers of Sir James Halkett's Regiment. There were also three troops of Morayshire cavalrymen under a Major Drummond. These probably represented the rump of Lord Gordon's Regiment that did not go over to the rebels in February. Campbell of Lawers may also have had a little troop of his own. In addition there were those 'dragooners' Hurry had picked up in Aberdeenshire, but they figure in none of the accounts of the battle and so presumably stayed safely in the rear. Discounting the latter, who were in any case no more than mounted infantry, it seems most unlikely that Hurry could muster

43

more than 300 cavalry and even some of these were of somewhat dubious quality. Neither Hurry nor the rebels had any artillery.

The rebel army was weaker still. The ever-meticulous Spalding claimed they were 3,000 strong, while Hurry reckoned, or at least assured his own men, that they had only about 2,000 infantry, besides 300 cavalry. On the other hand Montrose himself claimed to have had the staggeringly low total of only 1,400 men, both horse and foot. Astonishing as this figure sounds, it may not have been so very far from the truth, particularly since in the circumstances it seems likely that a good many of those who had been mustered with the army on the previous day never actually joined the fight.

James Fraser, who seems on the whole to be a reliable witness, credits Lord Gordon with having brought in 1,000 foot in addition to his 200 regular cavalry and Spalding agrees, adding 400 dragooners or mounted infantry. There were certainly two Gordon infantry regiments present, the veteran Strathbogie Regiment, and another newly raised one from Strathavan under William Gordon of Monymore. However, the latter only numbered some 200 men at Alford two months later, so it is unlikely that the two regiments actually mustered much more than 700 men between them, even if both regiments were present in their entirety, which seems unlikely. In addition there were probably no more than about 700 Irish and Highlanders under MacColla, although once again most of them were quartered well to the east of the village and he had no more than the 140 men of his lifeguard at hand when the battle began.

Auldearn: The castle hill viewed from the once marshy bottom as it may have been seen from the left flank of Lawers' brigade assaulting the village.

ORDER OF BATTLE
AULDEARN, 9 MAY 1645

ROYALISTS

Strathbogie Regiment	400
William Gordon of Monymore's Regiment	300
Irish companies	600
MacColla's Lifeguard	140
Lord Gordon's Horse	200
Viscount Aboyne's Horse	400

COVENANTERS

Regulars

Laird of Buchanan's Regiment (detachment)	200
Sir Mungo Campbell of Lawers' Regiment	400
Lord Chancellor's Regiment	400
Earl of Findlater's Regiment	300
Earl of Lothian's Regiment	400

Levies

Earl of Seaforth's Regiment	500
Earl of Sutherland's Regiment	500
Northern Levies	300+

Cavalry

Sir James Halkett's Regiment	160
Major Drummond's Troops	100
Campbell of Lawers' Troop	30

THE BATTLEFIELD

In 1644 the village of Auldearn was a straggle of cottages and yards built along a north–south axis on either side of the then road between Inverness and Forres. Confusingly the modern road cuts the village in half on an east–west axis. The growth of more modern building in the village has also been along this axis and consequently the battlefield itself is largely untouched. Generally speaking the village actually ran southwards from a point between the twin mounds marking a long-vanished motte and bailey castle on one side and a steep hill crowned by the church on the other. While some modern accounts speak of its lying along a low ridge-line, the old part of the village is actually situated on a terrace on the side of a westward-facing slope which then descends surprisingly sharply into a marshy 'bottom' formed by the Auldearn Burn and its feeders.

These small streams together with a fairly wide swathe of wet and boggy ground on each side formed a horseshoe, or rather almost a circle, enclosing a surprisingly prominent piece of relatively high ground called Garlic Hill, lying west-south-west of the village. This low hill, rising about 50ft above its immediate surroundings was perhaps of no great military significance in itself. It did, however, severely hamper the visibility of anyone not actually sitting on the top of it. In addition, and perhaps more

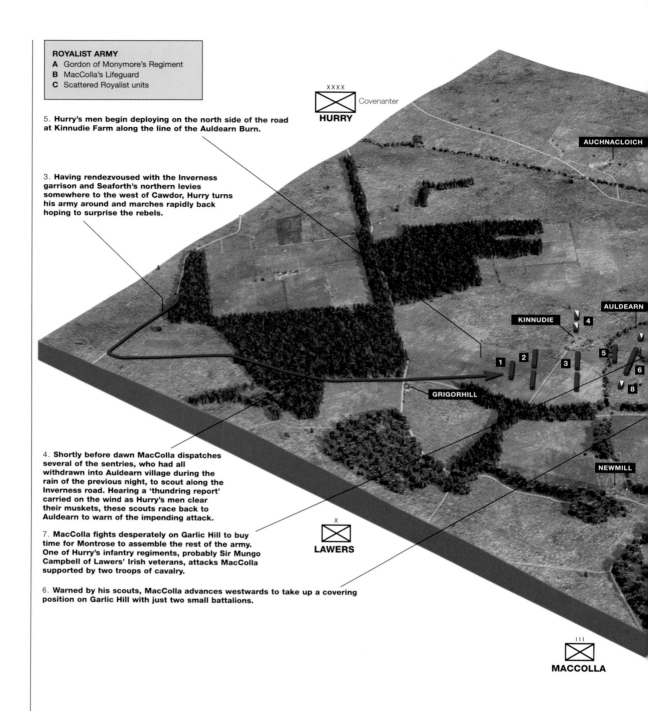

ROYALIST ARMY
A Gordon of Monymore's Regiment
B MacColla's Lifeguard
C Scattered Royalist units

xxxx
HURRY Covenanter

AUCHNACLOICH

5. Hurry's men begin deploying on the north side of the road at Kinnudie Farm along the line of the Auldearn Burn.

3. Having rendezvoused with the Inverness garrison and Seaforth's northern levies somewhere to the west of Cawdor, Hurry turns his army around and marches rapidly back hoping to surprise the rebels.

AULDEARN

KINNUDIE

GRIGORHILL

4. Shortly before dawn MacColla dispatches several of the sentries, who had all withdrawn into Auldearn village during the rain of the previous night, to scout along the Inverness road. Hearing a 'thundering report' carried on the wind as Hurry's men clear their muskets, these scouts race back to Auldearn to warn of the impending attack.

NEWMILL

7. MacColla fights desperately on Garlic Hill to buy time for Montrose to assemble the rest of the army. One of Hurry's infantry regiments, probably Sir Mungo Campbell of Lawers' Irish veterans, attacks MacColla supported by two troops of cavalry.

6. Warned by his scouts, MacColla advances westwards to take up a covering position on Garlic Hill with just two small battalions.

x
LAWERS

III
MACCOLLA

BATTLE OF AULDEARN –
MACCOLLA FIGHTING FOR TIME
9 May 1645, viewed from the south-east showing the rapid approach of Hurry's Covenanter army and Alasdair MacColla's desperate attempt to buy time while Montrose struggles to gather his scattered forces.

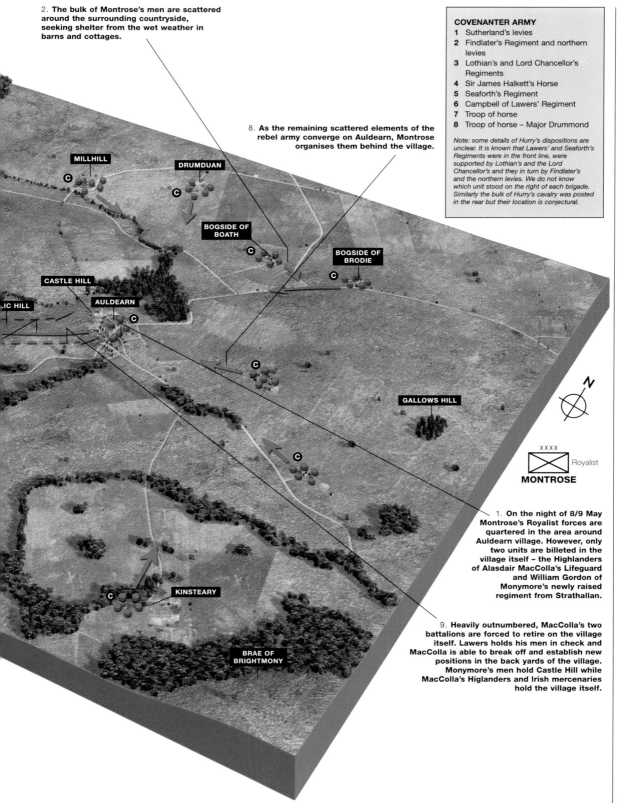

2. **The bulk of Montrose's men are scattered around the surrounding countryside, seeking shelter from the wet weather in barns and cottages.**

8. **As the remaining scattered elements of the rebel army converge on Auldearn, Montrose organises them behind the village.**

MILLHILL

DRUMDUAN

BOGSIDE OF BOATH

BOGSIDE OF BRODIE

CASTLE HILL

AULDEARN

IC HILL

GALLOWS HILL

xxxx
Royalist

MONTROSE

KINSTEARY

BRAE OF BRIGHTMONY

1. **On the night of 8/9 May Montrose's Royalist forces are quartered in the area around Auldearn village. However, only two units are billeted in the village itself – the Highlanders of Alasdair MacColla's Lifeguard and William Gordon of Monymore's newly raised regiment from Strathallan.**

9. **Heavily outnumbered, MacColla's two battalions are forced to retire on the village itself. Lawers holds his men in check and MacColla is able to break off and establish new positions in the back yards of the village. Monymore's men hold Castle Hill while MacColla's Higlanders and Irish mercenaries hold the village itself.**

crucially, it exerted a curious influence upon operations in that Hurry and his officers regarded it as being far more important than it actually was, and were consequently reluctant to stray off it. In 1645 it was partly covered in furze (gorse) bushes but is now quite bare. It is obvious from contemporary accounts of the battle that although the streams at its base did not, of themselves, constitute much of a military obstacle, the ground here was also a good deal wetter and boggier than in the present day. This may also have inhibited Hurry's men from moving off the hill. However, as events would show this low ground was easier to cross in some places than in others.

This was doubly unfortunate because Hurry, having turned northwards off the Inverness road to allow his men to clear their muskets, made no attempt to regain it. Instead of approaching the village along the axis of the road from the south, he marched directly across country in order to attack the village broadside on from the west, directly over the top of Garlic Hill. While the hill might appear a strong position it was a cramped area hemmed in by the marshy ground that was in turn enclosed by relatively high ground on three sides. None of this surrounding high ground was much higher, if at all, than Garlic Hill. However, as Hurry would discover to his cost it made his own deployment difficult and worse still completely masked what was happening on the far side.

EARLY MORNING

Meanwhile, hastily alerted by his scouts, Alasdair MacColla mustered every man he could find in the village and led them westward 'towards a marishe and som bushes, which was a strong ground and fencible against horsemen'. As he took up his position on top of Garlic Hill he discovered Hurry on the other side, deploying his own army at the farm of Kinnudie along the natural start-line of the Auldearn burn proper. At this point in time both forces were about 1/2 mile west of the village and MacColla knew he had to buy time for Montrose while he assembled the rest of the Royalist army.

It is difficult to be precise about how long this phase of the battle lasted. With two notable exceptions, contemporary accounts almost invariably compress the battle into a few sentences. This consequently creates the impression, inadvertently, that it was a fast-moving affair and all over very quickly. However, those accounts that do provide any sort of frame of reference are quite explicit in stating that the battle lasted all day. One report that reached Edinburgh stated that the fighting had raged for 12 hours. James Fraser, who left the only known account by one of Hurry's men, settles the matter, recording that the defeated army eventually withdrew across the river Nairn at How Ford, just two miles away from the battlefield, under cover of darkness. Consequently, the dramatic episodes recorded in the various accounts may represent quite extended periods of time interspersed by equally lengthy pauses in the fighting as each side regrouped for a renewed effort. Repeated reference is in fact made to 'long resistance' and 'continuall fire'.

In this initial phase of the battle MacColla was horribly outnumbered and immediately attacked by one of Hurry's regiments supported by two troops of horse. The infantry were almost certainly Sir Mungo Campbell

Auldearn: The broad top of the castle hill, held by Nathaniel Gordon and Monymore's Regiment. It is possible that Montrose may also have viewed the battle from here but there is no real evidence. The Boath Doocot was built during the 17th century but probably post-dates the battle.

of Lawers' veterans from Ireland. According to Fraser the rebels opened fire first but were soon getting the worst of the firefight. MacColla's own ensign was slain by the first volley and, although his distinctive yellow banner was immediately raised up again, three more men were shot down in quick succession while holding it aloft. 'So efter a brave and long maintained resistance, he is forced a reteir to som yards of the toun.'

As the rebels tumbled back Hurry prudently kept his men in check. He had made a promising start but MacColla's men only represented a detachment and until the rebels' main fighting line was developed he was understandably reluctant to commit his forces piecemeal. Consequently MacColla was able to break contact and take up a fresh

Auldearn: This photograph taken standing in the once marshy 'bottom' in front of the village clearly shows the comparative elevation of the village which must have made life very difficult for Lawers' men trying to break in.

CAMPBELL OF LAWERS' ATTACK ON AULDEARN VILLAGE
(pages 50–51)

During the opening stages of the battle the Royalist forward position on top of Garlic Hill was successfully stormed by the leading elements of Hurry's army and, getting the worst of the fire-fight, the outnumbered Royalists were forced to retire into the village of Auldearn itself (1). Once they had re-organised the Covenanters then moved forward with the intention of assaulting the village as well only for the attack to quite literally become bogged down. From the crest of the hill the village appears to be on much the same level but it is not immediately apparent that at its eastern end the hill falls away into what contemporaries referred to as a marshy 'bottom', forming a substantial natural ditch below the village (2). Consequently while the Highlanders and Irish mercenaries under Alasdair MacColla's personal command (3) scrambled to turn the small houses and back yards into a tenable defensive position, the attackers not only discovered that they had first to struggle across a muddy stream, but they were then faced with a surprisingly steep embankment rising up to the first of the houses. From there moreover the Royalists were able to pelt them with a heavy fire, and with Nathaniel Gordon's men firing into its flank as well the attack completely stalled and degenerated into a static fire-fight in which the Royalists, for the moment at least, held the upper hand. The failure of the initial assault was not from any want of determination on the part of the attackers for most of them belonged to Sir Mungo Campbell of Lawers' Regiment, one of seven recruited voluntarily by beat of drum rather than by conscription in 1642 for service against the Catholic rebels in Ulster (4). The war there was a particularly nasty affair, marked by atrocities on both sides and when any of the regiments subsequently recalled from there faced the Irish serving with the Royalists, black flags were figuratively hoisted and quarter neither given nor asked for, and so it was at Auldearn. Sir Mungo Campbell (5) was killed along with half of his officers and no doubt a similar proportion of the rank and file. Afterwards however Lawers' son, Sir James, rebuilt the regiment, chiefly from conscripts levied out of the Linlithgow area and it continued to give good service right through to the end of the war – a detachment taking part in Montrose's final defeat at Carbisdale in 1650. While Sir Mungo had originally raised a good many of his volunteers from the hills and glens of Perthshire the regiment was certainly not, as popularly believed, a Highland clan levy. Instead, as evidenced both by those recruits from Linlithgow and by records of weapons and ammunition issued, the regiment was equipped with pikes and matchlock muskets and clad in the ubiquitous hodden grey coats and breeches so characteristic of the Scots infantryman. (Gerry Embleton)

position in amongst the back yards of the village, which were significantly higher than the marshy ground at the base of the hill. The village was in fact a far stronger position than a casual reading of contemporary accounts would suggest. With the momentum of Lawers' attack slowed by the marshy ground and then stopped entirely by the steep slope, MacColla was able to make a stand. A fire-fight once again rippled up and down the line, described by one eyewitness as 'continuall shot'.

At least one (Highland) rebel account suggests that the two regiments under MacColla's command were completely intermingled at this point and that his own Irishmen and Highlanders were spread all along the line to prevent the raw Gordon recruits from running away. In the circumstances a certain amount of confusion and intermingling of personnel was no doubt inevitable, but the consensus actually seems to be that the village proper was largely held by MacColla's own men; a mixture of Irish mercenaries and his personal 'Lifeguard' of Highland kinsmen and friends. Nathaniel Gordon with Monymore's Regiment occupied the adjacent castle hill. The latter position was of crucial importance and quite literally the cornerstone of the defence. Not only was it strong enough to be easily defended in its own right but, since it projected westwards from the line of the village, Gordon's men were able to pour an effective fire into Lawers' left flank. There can, in fact, be little doubt that it was this flanking fire, as well as the unexpected steepness of the slope in front of him, that frustrated Lawers in his initial attempts to restore his men's momentum and push them up the embankment into the village.

In fact this combination was so effective that MacColla decided to mount a hasty counter-attack. Traditionally this move has been widely condemned by Montrose's apologists, who contend that MacColla's role was simply to hold Hurry's men in check while the Marquis positioned the remainder of his army for the decisive counter-attack. According to this interpretation MacColla foolishly jeopardised this cunning plan by advancing too soon and risking destruction before Montrose was ready.

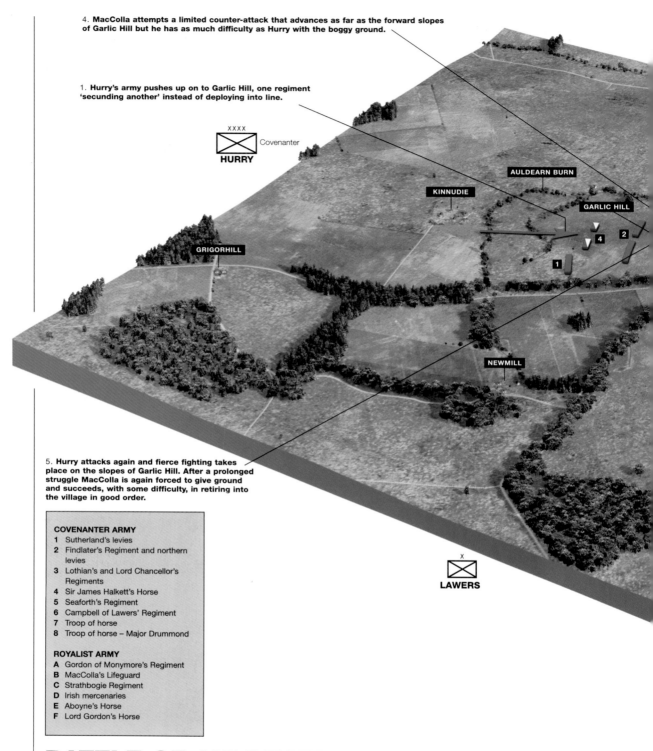

4. MacColla attempts a limited counter-attack that advances as far as the forward slopes of Garlic Hill but he has as much difficulty as Hurry with the boggy ground.

1. Hurry's army pushes up on to Garlic Hill, one regiment 'secunding another' instead of deploying into line.

XXXX
HURRY Covenanter

AULDEARN BURN

KINNUDIE

GARLIC HILL

GRIGORHILL

2

4

1

NEWMILL

5. Hurry attacks again and fierce fighting takes place on the slopes of Garlic Hill. After a prolonged struggle MacColla is again forced to give ground and succeeds, with some difficulty, in retiring into the village in good order.

x
LAWERS

COVENANTER ARMY
1 Sutherland's levies
2 Findlater's Regiment and northern levies
3 Lothian's and Lord Chancellor's Regiments
4 Sir James Halkett's Horse
5 Seaforth's Regiment
6 Campbell of Lawers' Regiment
7 Troop of horse
8 Troop of horse – Major Drummond

ROYALIST ARMY
A Gordon of Monymore's Regiment
B MacColla's Lifeguard
C Strathbogie Regiment
D Irish mercenaries
E Aboyne's Horse
F Lord Gordon's Horse

BATTLE OF AULDEARN – THE CRISIS

9 May 1645, viewed from the south-east showing the repeated attacks on Auldearn by Lawers' Brigade as they attempt to overrun MacColla's outnumbered defenders. In the meantime the bulk of the Royalist army is forming up behind the village itself.

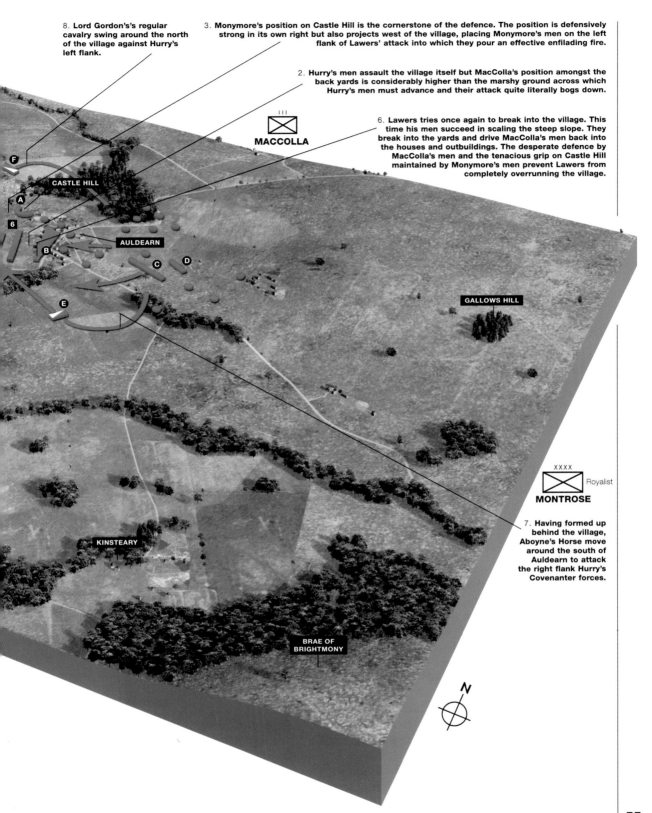

8. Lord Gordon's's regular cavalry swing around the north of the village against Hurry's left flank.

3. Monymore's position on Castle Hill is the cornerstone of the defence. The position is defensively strong in its own right but also projects west of the village, placing Monymore's men on the left flank of Lawers' attack into which they pour an effective enfilading fire.

2. Hurry's men assault the village itself but MacColla's position amongst the back yards is considerably higher than the marshy ground across which Hurry's men must advance and their attack quite literally bogs down.

6. Lawers tries once again to break into the village. This time his men succeed in scaling the steep slope. They break into the yards and drive MacColla's men back into the houses and outbuildings. The desperate defence by MacColla's men and the tenacious grip on Castle Hill maintained by Monymore's men prevent Lawers from completely overrunning the village.

MACCOLLA

CASTLE HILL

F
A
6
B
AULDEARN
C
D
E

GALLOWS HILL

MONTROSE Royalist

7. Having formed up behind the village, Aboyne's Horse move around the south of Auldearn to attack the right flank Hurry's Covenanter forces.

KINSTEARY

BRAE OF BRIGHTMONY

N

Auldearn: Garlic Hill as seen from the top of the castle hill – Kinnudie can just be seen at the extreme right of the photograph. This graphically illustrates how Monymore's men were able to bring down an effective flanking fire of the men moving off Garlic Hill to attack the village.

In reality there was no carefully thought out ambush in preparation and no evidence at all that Montrose, or anyone else, ordered MacColla to remain on the defensive inside the village. The Royalists had been surprised and Montrose had more than enough to contend with pulling his scattered army together, without dreaming up a brilliant (but quite unforeseen) ambush. Until such time as he could assemble and bring forward the rest of the army MacColla was on his own. It was up to him to fight the battle as best he could. Having decisively halted Lawers' advance, a local counter-attack at this point was entirely appropriate, particularly as ammunition may have been running low.

Assuming that first light in the overcast conditions would have been around 7.00am, it is likely that the battle proper did not begin until sometime between 8.00 and 9.00am. This could mean that MacColla did not repulse the first attack on the village until 10.00am. Given the time necessary to organise the counter-attack, this may not have been launched much before 11.00am.

The counter-attack began promisingly enough but then, quite literally, got bogged down in the same marshy bottom that had slowed Lawers' attack in the first place. Patrick Gordon of Ruthven, who was evidently an eyewitness, explicitly stated that 'the ground wpon his left hand being all quagmyre and bushes, was in this second charge extreamly to his dissadvantage, wher his men could nether advance in order, not fynd sure footing to stand, nor marche forward to helpe ther fellows.'

Clearly, therefore, this was no wild and impetuous Highland charge, or else Ruthven would not have stressed the difficulty of advancing 'in order' or, more critically, of bringing the left wing up to support the centre and right, which appear to have fought their way up on to the forward slopes of Garlic Hill. Lawers, for his part, retired back up to the top of the hill, reorganised and then counter-attacked in turn, this time with two regiments. Once again however this must have taken some time

OPPOSITE **Auldearn: Aboyne's cavalry formed up on the other side of the low ridge marked by the further line of trees, then attacked the right wing of Hurry's army just forward of the houses at the left. Afterwards the Strathbogie Regiment attacked from the direction of the houses towards the camera.**

to organise. Indeed both common-sense and an overwhelming weight of precedent from countless similar episodes in military history would indicate that it took approximately an hour to get everyone in place.

This attack, which probably took place around midday, was much better co-ordinated than the initial Covenanter assault. Once again Lawers' own veterans led the attack. Many of Seaforth's Highland levies were armed with bows and so Lawers seems to have positioned them behind his regiment in order that they could shoot over their heads to provide both indirect fire on the objective and to try to do something to suppress the deadly flanking fire from the castle hill.

Perhaps for that reason this second attack was, ultimately, more successful: 'The enemie, coming wp two regiments in a full body, flanked with horsemen, did charge the major [MacColla] in that deficult place; and the rest of ther maine battell following, on[e] regiment still secunding ane other; yet efter a strong and absteinat resistance, he maintenes his station with invinceible curage a long tym, till, opprest with multitude, and charge wpon charge, he was forced to give ground, and with great deficulty, befor he could reteir his people in good order, or kepe them from confuised fleight.'

The salient points that emerge from all of this are that the fighting on the hill was once again prolonged and that, albeit with some difficulty, MacColla eventually succeeded in retiring in good order back into the village. All of the Royalist accounts place great emphasis on the hand-to-hand fighting at this stage in the battle. This points, albeit obliquely, to MaColla's men having practically exhausted their ammunition, although one must set Ruthven's account, which emphasises the continued heavy firing, against this.

This time Lawers' men finally got up the steep slope, broke into the yards and drove MacColla's men back into the houses and outbuildings

One of a number of Highland mercenaries sketched by Köler in Stettin in 1631. He appears to be armed only with a bow, but almost certainly carries a dirk as well on his left hip.

Auldearn: Having swung wide of the castle hill, Lord Gordon crossed over the low ridge line marked by the gorse bushes and trees in the middle distance to attack the left wing of Hurry's army extending down the slope of Garlic Hill below the camera.

from where they maintained a furious, and often hand-to-hand resistance. Gaelic chroniclers afterwards eulogised this part of the battle, oblivious to the equally desperate stand by Monymore's men on the castle hill, who continued to fire into Lawers' flank all the while. Instead it was Alasdair and his swordsmen alone who were the heroes, not the allegedly cowardly Gordons: Alasdair … you were good that day at Auldearn, when you leapt among the pikes; and whether good or ill befell you, you would not shout 'Relief'. Hemmed in by Lawers' men, MacColla had a number of pikes thrust into his round targe, but hacked off their heads, only for his sword to break in his hand. Ruthven rather picturesquely claims that he actually 'brak two swords' after which he was handed a third by his brother-in-law, Davidson of Applecross who, in the best heroic tradition, was then cut down himself. As Applecross died, MacColla regained the temporary safety of a doorway, covered by another of his men, named Ranald Mackinnon. Mackinnon pistolled an over-eager pikemen but then had an arrow shot through both his cheeks. Dropping the empty pistol Mackinnon tried to draw his sword, only to find it had stuck in the scabbard. He then received a number of superficial wounds before staggering into the house. According to the bards a pikemen tried to follow him, but as he stuck his head through the door MacColla promptly cut it off. MacColla was, we are told, all the while cursing the Gordons who he thought had let him down, although in reality it was probably only their tenacious grip on the castle hill that was preventing Lawers from completely overrunning the village.

Nevertheless although Lawers could not get his cavalry over the dykes and into the village his infantry alone were sufficient to do the business. The pressure was simply becoming too great and, in what must have been a brief pause as Lawers marshalled his men for the final assault, MacColla recognised that a total collapse was perhaps only a matter of minutes away.

'… then for griefe was he ready to burst, seeing non to second him, and saw no hope of victorie, but all the simptoms of a disasterous and dreadful overthrow. Wherefor he called to those that wer about him, "Ach, messoures," said he, "sall our enemies by this on dayes work be able to wreast out of our handes all the glorie that we have formerly gained. Let it never be said that a basse flight shall bear witness of it, or that our actiones should seem to confesse so much; but let us die bravely; let it never be thought that they have triumphed over our courage, nor the loyaltie we ow to our soveraigne lord, and let us hope the best. God is stronge enough." And whill he whispered these words for he would not speak aloud, least the enemies might imagine of yielding, behold how gratious Heavin and the Devyne Power did assist him.'

THE REBEL COUNTER-ATTACKS BEGIN

The crisis of the battle had now been reached. MacColla, however tenuously, still held the village and Nathaniel Gordon the castle hill, but only just. Hurry's army, meanwhile, had still not deployed into a battle-line but was largely stacked up behind Lawers' Brigade on Garlic Hill 'on[e] regiment still secunding ane other' as Ruthven put it. Unfortunately, with his attention clearly fixed on the fight for the village, Hurry was quite unaware of what was happening beyond it.

All this time Montrose and his officers had been desperately mustering the rest of the rebel army. Traditionally he is said to have concealed his men a little to the south of the village, in an area subsequently known as 'Montrose's Hollow', in preparation for a bold counter-attack, only to see MacColla defeated and driven back into the village. Fearing the worst, he then retrieved the situation handsomely by telling Lord Gordon, quite falsely, that MacColla was driving all before him and inviting the cavalry to emulate his success before he snatched all the glory. Gordon, it is said, then charged forward and saved the day by completely routing Hurry's forces.

What actually happened was rather less straightforward, for it is clear that there were at least three quite different attacks launched during the course of the afternoon. In his own very brief report on the battle, Montrose himself simply said that 'the enemy being confident both of their men and their number fell hotly on, but being beat back, seimed to coole of their fury, and only intended to blocke us up (as it wer) till more number should come which perceiving I divided myselfe in two wings (which was all the ground would suffer) and marched upon them most unexpectedly.' This can be read to mean that, while MacColla held the village with one 'wing' of the army, Montrose counter-attacked with the other. A much more convincing interpretation, and one explicitly confirmed by Ruthven, is that because the broken nature of the ground prevented him from forming a conventional battle-line, Montrose instead divided the forces he had mustered behind the village into two separate wings and directed one wing around the north end of it and the other around the south side.

By this time Montrose must have assembled as many of his men as he was ever going to gather. The apparently piecemeal nature of the series

Auldearn: The original church, the nearer of the two sections seen in the photo, was extended in the 1750s with the addition of the structure seen in the background. The roof of the original church appears to have been moved to the newer building. Many of those killed in the battle were buried here. Montrose almost certainly lodged in the adjacent manse on the night before the battle.

of attacks that followed must have been dictated by the desperate need to relieve the pressure on MacColla's beleaguered men. If Montrose did dupe his cavalry into attacking, the deception must have been perpetrated not on Lord Gordon, but on his younger brother Aboyne. It was he who, attacking from the south, launched the first charge against Lawers' right flank. Ruthven, whose account of the battle is far and away the most detailed, related that 'They receive his charge with such a continuall giving of fire, as he seemed, by the thick smok throw which he went, to assalt a terrible cloud of thunder and lightening'. It seems much more likely that the smoke and fury was directed at the defenders of the village and that Aboyne's approach was effectively hidden from the Covenanters until it was too late. The result was devastating. Lawers' flank was supposedly covered by one of two troops of horse under a Major Drummond. He promptly panicked and, ordering his men to wheel to the left rather than to the right, avoided combat by riding over his own infantry.

Aboyne followed him into the shattered ranks and took four or five colours, although from which of Hurry's regiments this might have been is unknown. It was evidently not Lawers' men for they were still fighting their way into the village. It is possible the colours were taken from Seaforth's men, but more likely it was some of Hurry's anonymous regulars. It may have been the Lord Chancellor's Regiment, which was particularly badly cut up in the battle. The charge certainly relieved the pressure on the village, for Lawers broke off the attack and started retiring back up the eastern slope of Garlic Hill. It was at this point that Lord Gordon appeared to the north from behind the castle hill, leading his own regular cavalry regiment:

'My Lord Gordon by this time charges the left winge', said Ruthven, 'and that with a new form of fight, for he discharges all shooting of pistoles and carrabines, only with ther swords to charge quhyt throwgh ther enemies, who wer so many in number, and so stronge and weell horsed as if by a desperat charge they had got them not broken, it was too apparent that they might recover the day. But Aboyn having overthrowen the right winge, and the main battell left bair on that syd, and seing Montrose and McDonnell joyned to give a new charge, the great body began to stagger, all their hopes being in ther left winge; and that my lord Gordon charges so soundly with swords only, as if they scorned to be resisted; they had all sworn to go throw or dye.'

Having summarily disposed of the single troop of horse on the left wing, Gordon charged straight into the flank of the unfortunate infantry, presumably Lawers' retreating brigade. He evidently drove the fugitives southwards as, according to Fraser the one known eyewitness in the ranks of Hurry's army, many of them were killed around the farms of Kinsteary and Brightmony nearly a mile to the south-east of the village.

VICTORY

In the meantime Hurry could only brace himself to meet a renewed assault by the Royalist infantry. Fraser vividly recalled the horror of those standing on Garlic Hill as they saw the Strathbogie Regiment sweep around the southern end of the village.

Accounts of this final stage of the battle, as the Royalists stormed up on to Garlic Hill for the third time, are tantalisingly brief but it was evidently a savage fight. Montrose, laconic as ever, relates only that there were 'some hot salvyes of musket and a litell dealing with sword and pike.' All of the other chroniclers emphasise the sheer ferocity of the fighting. Spalding states that Hurry's men were 'for the most part cut af, fighting to the death most valiauntlie', while Fraser sorrowfully described how the rebels 'run throw them, killing and goaring under foot … Lairs and Lothians regiment stood in their ranks and files, and were so killed as they stood.' Ruthven recalled that 'you should have sein how the infantrie of the Royalists, keiping together and following the charge of the horsemen, did tear and cut them in pieces, even in rankes and fyles, as they stood, so great was the execution which they made efter the horse had shanken and quyt astonished them, by persueing rudly throw them, as it was very lamentable to behold.'

As the situation fell apart, Hurry withdrew westwards with his cavalry and probably a fair number of his surviving infantry as well. The Inverness road was evidently swarming with Royalist cavalrymen by this time. There was momentary confusion in the gathering dusk, however, when Lord Gordon's men mistook Aboyne's troopers for the enemy. Hurry took the opportunity to strike off the main road and head due west across country. He eventually got the remnants of his army safely across the River Nairn that night a couple of miles west of the battlefield at Howford. The reason for this fortuitous confusion was that Aboyne's men were proudly displaying the colours they had captured.

Whilst the Royalists, as usual, claimed to have slain their opponents in biblical numbers it is possible on this occasion to be a little more particular about the numbers lost by both sides. Campbell of Lawers' Regiment lost its colonel, lieutenant-colonel (William Campbell) and at least four of the company commanders – Captain Campbell, Captain

THE STRATHBOGIE REGIMENT COUNTER-ATTACKS
(pages 62–63)

James Fraser, the only known eyewitness in the ranks of Hurry's army, recorded the dismay of the soldiers standing on top of Garlic Hill as they saw the large Strathbogie Regiment, perhaps 500 strong, suddenly sweeping around the southern end of the village and driving up the slope towards them. It was by Civil War standards a veteran regiment which had originally been raised or rather levied by the Marquis of Huntly in the far north-east of Scotland away back in 1639. As well as ensuring that it was properly equipped with muskets and pikes (1) in the recommended proportion of 2:1 out of a supply sent from Hull by the King, Huntly also employed professional soldiers such as Nathaniel Gordon to train it. Consequently it performed well in the very first battle of the Civil wars at Turriff on 14 May 1639 and afterwards at Megray Hill and the Brig o' Dee. Disbanded after the Pacification of Berwick, it was raised afresh by Huntly in the spring of 1644, occupied Aberdeen and raided the burgh of Montrose, and was again called out by his son Lord Gordon after his defection to the Royalists early in 1645. It then went on to fight at Dundee, Auldearn, Alford, Kilsyth and in the final battle – Huntly's storming of Aberdeen on 14 May 1646, seven years to the day since they had fought in the first at Turriff. Although raised from amongst the Gordons, their tenants and their followers, it was not a Highland clan levy. Strathbogie had traditionally bred good pikemen such as the two companies the then Earl of Huntly had recruited for the French service in 1552 'substantiouslie accompturit with jack and plait, steilbonnet, sword, bucklair ... and a speir of sax elne long [16ft] or thairby'. Contemporary chroniclers such as Spalding and Ruthven were therefore careful to distinguish between the Strathbogie men and Huntly's wilder clan levies from Upper Deeside and beyond, and Spalding in particular noted seeing a detachment of 'about 60 muskiteiris and pikoneiris, with twa cullouris, ane drum (2), and ane bag pipe' in April 1644. The colours shown here (3) were also made in Aberdeen at that time – see black and white illustrations. It is unclear, however, who actually commanded the regiment at Auldearn. It may have been Major Nathaniel Gordon, who spent much of the battle defending the crucial castle hill position, but he normally served with the cavalry and it is likely that the Strathbogie Regiment was actually led by Major or Lieutenant-Colonel John Gordon of Littlemill (4). At any rate Littlemill afterwards recorded that he had marched with Montrose and Huntly 'first as ane captane, then as Major and last as Lieutenant collonell' from Inverlochy to Aberdeen. (Gerry Embleton)

William Bruce, Captain Cashore and Captain Shaw. All six of them, together with five lieutenants and 200 men, were afterwards buried at Cawdor, a Campbell seat. The fact that the church lies some six miles from the battlefield suggests most of the latter may have been wounded men and fugitives from a variety of units. While it suffered badly the regiment was far from destroyed as in February 1646 its officers complained that they had been in garrison at Inverness since October 1644 and only received a half month's pay in all that time!

The losses of the Earl of Lothian's Regiment must have been similar. It again lost four company commanders – Captain William Douglas (presumably one of the nine nephews of Douglas of Cavers said to have been killed there), Captain Alexander Drummond, Captain Gideon Murray and Captain Sir John Murray. The latter three were buried in Auldearn church along with a Captain Crichton who probably belonged to Findlater's Regiment. Both Findlater and his lieutenant-colonel, Walter Ogilvie of Boyne, escaped from the battlefield but nothing further is heard of his regiment, which presumably disintegrated. Worst hit may have been the Lord Chancellor's Regiment, for a bare 100 men survived to fight at Kilsyth in August.

The various northern levies also appear to have suffered quite badly. It is probable that they scattered more readily than the regulars once the rout began and so were more vulnerable, although the evidence for this is largely anecdotal. Robert Grant, the eldest son of Grant of Shewglie in Glen Urquhart, was killed as was a Captain Bernard McKenzie together with most of his company from the Chanonry of Ross in the Black Isle. Fraser recorded that his own chief, Lovat, was left with 87 widows to support and presumably not all of those who died were married.

Rebel losses may not have been so very much lighter. Ruthven rather airily quotes 16 dead, 14 of them MacColla's men, while Spalding gives '24 gentlemen hurt to Montross, and sum few Irishes killit, which is miraculous'. The significant word however is gentlemen, which to all intents and purposes may be translated as officers. Gordon of Sallagh, on the other hand, while recording 22 gentlemen killed (which is broadly consistent with both Ruthven's and Spalding's accounts) rather more realistically adds 200 common soldiers killed. Added to this must be an unknown number of wounded. The fact that, shortly afterwards, it took a whole day to get the baggage train and wounded across the Spey and into the relative security of Bog of Gight Castle gives some idea of just how many wounded there were.

There is no doubt that this pyrrhic victory had crippled the Royalist army. Instead of pursuing Hurry's men and moving on Inverness Montrose retreated eastwards. Nevertheless, although the victory had been very dearly bought, it remained a victory and effectively neutralised the government's northern forces.

Auldearn: Memorial in the old church to Alexander Drummond, Sir John Murray and Gideon Murray, officers in Lothian's Regiment who were killed in the battle and buried in the church. Interestingly the memorial states that they fell 'fighting walliantly in defence of ther Rellegion, King and Native Covntry'.

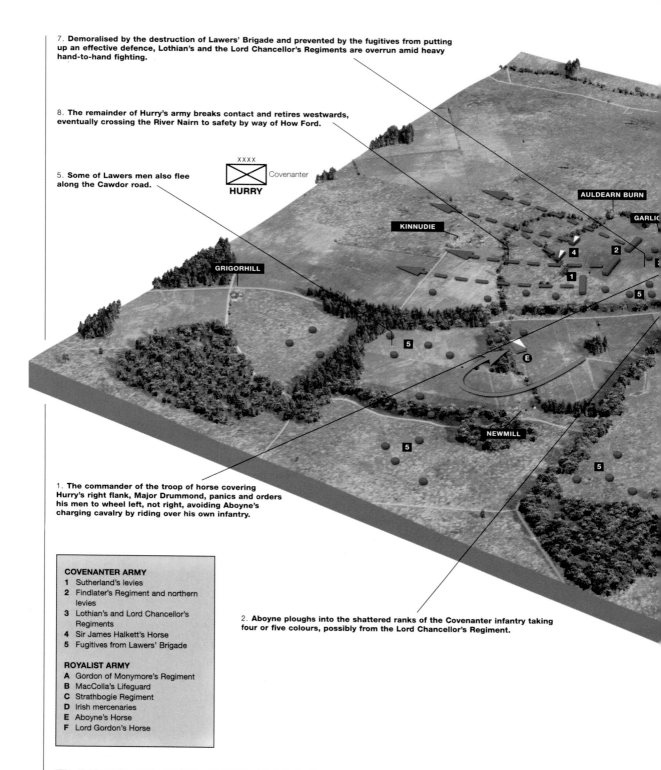

7. Demoralised by the destruction of Lawers' Brigade and prevented by the fugitives from putting up an effective defence, Lothian's and the Lord Chancellor's Regiments are overrun amid heavy hand-to-hand fighting.

8. The remainder of Hurry's army breaks contact and retires westwards, eventually crossing the River Nairn to safety by way of How Ford.

5. Some of Lawers men also flee along the Cawdor road.

XXXX
Covenanter
HURRY

AULDEARN BURN

GARLIC

KINNUDIE

GRIGORHILL

NEWMILL

1. The commander of the troop of horse covering Hurry's right flank, Major Drummond, panics and orders his men to wheel left, not right, avoiding Aboyne's charging cavalry by riding over his own infantry.

COVENANTER ARMY
1 Sutherland's levies
2 Findlater's Regiment and northern levies
3 Lothian's and Lord Chancellor's Regiments
4 Sir James Halkett's Horse
5 Fugitives from Lawers' Brigade

ROYALIST ARMY
A Gordon of Monymore's Regiment
B MacColla's Lifeguard
C Strathbogie Regiment
D Irish mercenaries
E Aboyne's Horse
F Lord Gordon's Horse

2. Aboyne ploughs into the shattered ranks of the Covenanter infantry taking four or five colours, possibly from the Lord Chancellor's Regiment.

BATTLE OF AULDEARN – VICTORY

9 May 1645, viewed from the south-east showing the destruction of Lawers' Brigade by the Royalist cavalry and the decisive counter-attack by Montrose's infantry, which sweeps Hurry's Covenanter's off Garlic Hill in disarray.

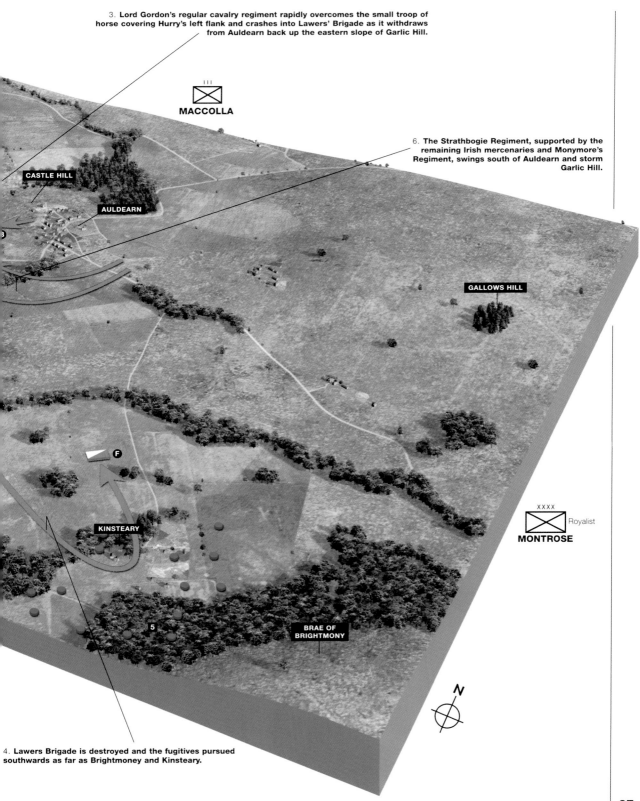

3. **Lord Gordon's regular cavalry regiment rapidly overcomes the small troop of horse covering Hurry's left flank and crashes into Lawers' Brigade as it withdraws from Auldearn back up the eastern slope of Garlic Hill.**

MACCOLLA

6. **The Strathbogie Regiment, supported by the remaining Irish mercenaries and Monymore's Regiment, swings south of Auldearn and storm Garlic Hill.**

CASTLE HILL

AULDEARN

GALLOWS HILL

F

KINSTEARY

xxxx
Royalist

MONTROSE

BRAE OF BRIGHTMONY

5

N

4. **Lawers Brigade is destroyed and the fugitives pursued southwards as far as Brightmoney and Kinsteary.**

THE CAMPAIGN CONTINUES

The day after the battle the rebels returned to Elgin, which they plundered thoroughly before falling back still further. Re-crossing the Spey, they rested for a few days at Birkenbog near Cullen, where they engaged in plundering and burning the Earl of Findlater's lands. Meanwhile Baillie was on the move. Delayed by a fruitless raid into Atholl, he had resolved to re-unite his own forces with those sent north under Hurry and crossed the Dee near Birse only to receive unconfirmed reports of a battle on 11 May. At this point he had only 800 Foot and 100 Horse, the remainder of his army having been left behind to watch the passes. Not unnaturally he halted at Tarland to wait for reinforcements. These turned up a week later in the shape of the Earl of Balcarres at the head of his own veteran regiment of cavalry and two ad hoc battalions of 'redcoats'. The latter, under the command of Colonel Robert Home, were drawn from the regiments of the Scots army in Ulster. Even with this solid reinforcement he was inclined to be wary since he lacked reliable intelligence of the rebels' whereabouts. This was remedied when Sir John Hurry broke out of Inverness with his remaining cavalry on 20 May.

At that point the balance of affairs abruptly shifted. Not only did Baillie now know exactly where the rebels were, but for the first time he also learned that their curious and quite uncharacteristic inactivity proceeded from their heavy losses in the battle. Moreover, widely dispersed as they were, they were clearly vulnerable to a sudden offensive – and so it proved. On 21 May Montrose received 'haistie advertesment' that Baillie was marching north from Cocklarochie. His initial reaction was to move forward with whatever troops were immediately at hand. He began digging

Tolquhon Castle near Udny in Aberdeenshire; Walter Forbes of Tolquhon was a prominent adherent of the Covenant, held the castle against Huntly's men early in 1644 and afterwards fought in the Craibstane Rout at Aberdeen.

The ford over the river Don at Mountgarrie crossed by Baillie's army in its advance to contact on the morning of 2 July 1645. The Royalist position on Gallows Hill is marked by the tree-crowned hill in the left distance.

in at Strathbogie (Huntly) Castle that evening. However, later that night he decided discretion was, after all, the better part of valour and hastily decamped westwards to Balvenie on Speyside.

Baillie was soon on the rebels' trail and caught up with them at Glenlivet, showing his troops must have been marching hard. The rebels shook him off again at nightfall, however. Next morning Baillie's scouts deduced by the trampled grass and heather that the rebel army was making for Abernethy on Speyside. Setting off again he seems to have caught up with them somewhere near Aviemore 'in the entrie of Badzenoch, a very strait country, where, both for unaccessible rocks, woods, and the interposition of the river, it wes impossible for us to come at them'.

Reluctantly he had to admit defeat. His men had done all that was asked of them and more, but now they were exhausted and starving, the cavalry complaining that they had had no food for 48 hours. With the rebels posted in an unassailable position, Baillie had no alternative but to pull back to Inverness and refit.

As soon as Baillie had marched out of sight Montrose sought to capitalise on his isolation by lunging southwards, hoping to break out of the hills into the seemingly undefended Lowlands. Instead the rebels found themselves confronted by another force under the Earl of Crawford-Lindsay[1], dug in along the river Isla at Newtyle in Angus. Whatever hopes Montrose might have entertained of forcing this position were then abruptly dashed by the news that Baillie had moved out of Inverness and was devastating the Gordon recruiting grounds in the north-east. Lord Gordon thereupon headed north with all his men, leaving Montrose with just 200-odd Irish mercenaries and no alternative but to retreat back into the hills.

Baillie meanwhile had crossed the Spey and rendezvoused with Crawford-Lindsay at Drum Castle near Aberdeen. The Earl brought bad news. The Committee of Estates was dissatisfied with his handling of operations and rather astonishingly considered him to be insufficiently determined in his pursuit of the rebels! Instead a new army was to be

---

1 Originally simply known as John, Earl of Lindsay, he became the Earl of Crawford-Lindsay after the attainder of a Royalist officer, Ludovick Lindsay, Earl of Crawford. Confusingly the latter was still alive and well at the time and subsequently served under Montrose against Crawford-Lindsay.

ABOVE **Only the central portion of this all-white colonel's colour was captured at Dunbar or rather more likely at Inverkeithing. The surviving lettering is black, the uncoloured lettering being reconstructed. It was carried there by Forbes of Leslie, but the old Religion For Covenant King and Cuntrie motto indicates that it may originally have been carried by the regiment raised in Aberdeenshire by Lord Forbes in 1644. At least part of the regiment may have fought at Alford under Forbes of Leslie since Baillie picked up the surviving Aberdeenshire forces at Leslie Castle on the day before.**

ABOVE, RIGHT **Alford: Gallows Hill as seen from Baillie's position below. The top of the hill is now crowned with trees but the centre and left wing of the Royalist army appears to have been drawn up along the prominent but slightly lower ridge line clearly seen in this photograph.**

formed under the Marquis of Argyle and Baillie, now relegated to a purely defensive supporting role, was ordered to give up his own 'Irish' brigade (the 1,200 veterans drawn from the Scots army in Ulster under Colonel Robert Home) and 100 of Balcarres' Horse in exchange for a mere 400 men of the Earl of Cassillis's Regiment of Foot.

This nonsensical plan was soon abandoned. First Argyle refused command of the new army and then Crawford-Lindsay went off with it on a pointless expedition into Atholl. Baillie meanwhile, far from remaining on the defensive, was ordered to take his badly depleted little army back into rebel territory and rendezvous with the Earl of Seaforth. Unfortunately, despite receiving a substantial shipment of muskets and pikes with which to equip his new levies, Seaforth failed to make the rendezvous on Speyside. General Baillie was falling back on Aberdeen when he ran into the rebels at Keith on 24 June. Fortunately, having had some warning of their approach he took up a good position by the church and the discomfited rebels were once again reduced to challenging him to come down and fight them in the open. Naturally enough he refused and to his surprise they immediately began retreating southwards. Intrigued he sent his scouts out again and discovered that the invitation to fight at Keith had been a bluff. Alasdair MacColla was absent with his men and the rebels were just as weak as he was. Setting off after them he came in sight of the rebels at the foot of the Coreen Hills, some distance to the north of Alford. There Montrose turned at bay on some rising ground either at the Suie Foot or Knockespock. Baillie declined to fight and 'turned aside about three miles to the left' to rendezvous with the Aberdeenshire forces at Leslie Castle. Greatly relieved, Montrose then hastily decamped down the Suie road to Alford.

THE BATTLE OF ALFORD

The morning of 2 July 1645 found the rebel army posted on top of a large, rounded eminence known as Gallows Hill, just to the south of the swift-flowing river Don. That much is certain, but there is some considerable dispute as to where the battle was actually fought. The generally accepted

Alford: The Royalist right wing was initially positioned along this sky-line before advancing down the gentle slope towards the camera.

version of events in secondary sources is that Baillie followed the Royalists down the Suie Road, crossed the Don at Boat of Forbes directly to the north of Gallows Hill and mistaking the rebel forces posted thereon for a rearguard, rashly tried to push past only to have them descend upon his men like the proverbial wolf on the fold.

According to a contemporary Aberdeenshire ballad (evidently written by one of the unfortunate Forbes levies), having spent the night at Leslie, Baillie in fact marched due south parallel to, but some distance to the east of, the Suie Road. Furthermore, far from rushing blindly in pursuit of the rebels, the ballad specifically relates that Baillie formed his men in order of battle at Mill Hill. This is a farm lying on the road that crosses the Correen Hills between Knock Soul and Satter Hill, near where it comes down to cross the Don by the ford at Mountgarrie. This ford lies about a mile downstream from Boat of Forbes and the fact that Baillie formed his men in order of battle before crossing at Mountgarrie confirms that he was deliberately advancing to contact, not from the north, but from the east. Nevertheless, recognising that the rebels held a strong position on top of the hill, once he was across Baillie halted on the low-lying How of Alford.

Baillie's army can be partially reconstructed both by reference to his own report and other official papers. He had at least six regiments of regulars – Cassillis's, Elcho's, Lanark's, Moray's, Glencairn's and Callendar's – of which the first at least mustered about 400 men. The probability is that in total he had about 2,400 infantry although it is possible that there may also have been a seventh regiment, made up of Aberdeenshire levies. Baillie himself reckoned that he was outnumbered by about 2:1 and rather unusually drew his men up only three ranks deep to avoid their being outflanked.

As to the cavalry protecting those flanks, Baillie makes reference only to Balcarres' Regiment on the left and Halkett's Regiment on the right totalling a mere 260 men. However the Royalist accounts, perhaps predictably, credit him with twice that number and it is probably significant that Baillie also refers to his regiments being drawn up in three squadrons rather than the two that was the normal practice in the Scots army. Presumably therefore the additional squadrons were some of the

RELIGION

for the   Covenant

King and Kingdome

This colour was one of a number carried by Forbes of Leslie's Regiment in 1650 although the archaic motto indicates it was originally used by Lord Forbes' Regiment in 1644. It is green with a yellow saltire, gold lettering and a stag's head depicted naturally.

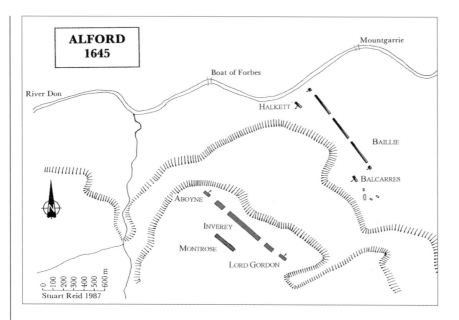

ALFORD
1645

Mountgarrie

Boat of Forbes

River Don

HALKETT

BAILLIE

BALCARRES

ABOYNE

INVEREY

MONTROSE

LORD GORDON

0 -100 -200 -300 -400 -500 -600 m

Stuart Reid 1987

Initial dispositions at the battle of Alford. The present village is largely a product of the railway age and in 1645 was represented only by a small scatter of cottages adjacent to Balcarres' position. Both sides moved forward to meet in the centre of the field.

Aberdeenshire troops picked up at Leslie the day before and Baillie may therefore have had something approaching 400 cavalry in all.

The composition of the rebel army is not quite so clear. Notwithstanding Baillie's claim to have been outnumbered, there is fairly broad agreement that they disposed of some 200–300 cavalry commanded by Lord Gordon and his brother Aboyne, and something over 2,000 infantry.

According to Ruthven the main battle or centre comprised the Strathbogie Regiment and 'Huntly's Highlanders' – a rather elastic term that certainly encompassed James Farquharson of Inverey's 'standing regiment' as well as William Gordon of Monymore's Strathavan men. In total the Gordon contingent must have been about 1,000 strong. To all intents and purposes it was made up of regulars, or at least veterans who could be relied upon to do what they were told by Inverey, who had the command of the whole. Oddly enough, however, Montrose's chaplain,

Alford: The battlefield as seen from the centre of the Royalist start line. The flat and open nature of the How of Alford is readily apparent.

George Wishart, claimed that MacDonald of Glengarry commanded the centre. While Ruthven explicitly denied this statement, it does point to the surprising presence of a MacDonald contingent that may have added around another 200 to the front line.

Since Baillie clearly had more cavalry than the Royalists, the remaining Irish mercenaries were parcelled out on the wings to support the rebel cavalry – Laghtnan's Regiment with Lord Gordon on the right and O'Cahan's with Aboyne on the left. In addition there was also a reserve placed behind the centre under the command of Lord Napier, although its composition is uncertain.

ORDER OF BATTLE
ALFORD, 2 JULY 1645

ROYALISTS

Strathbogie Regiment	500
Colonel James Farquharson of Inverey's Regiment	300
Colonel William Gordon of Monymore's Regiment	200
MacDonalds of Glengarry	200
Irish companies	600

Cavalry

Lord Gordon's Regiment	200
Viscount Aboyne's Regiment	300

COVENANTERS

Earl of Callendar's Regiment	
Earl of Cassillis' Regiment	
Lord Elcho's Regiment	
Earl of Glencairn's Regiment	
Earl of Lanark's Regiment	
Earl of Moray's Regiment	
Colonel George Forbes of Millbuie's Regiment(?)	
	Total: 2,400

Earl of Balcarres' Horse } Sir James Halkett's Horse	260
Sir William Forbes of Craigievar's Horse } John Forbes of Leslie's Horse Master of Forbes' Horse	120

Understandably enough, Baillie was far from keen on the idea of attacking and afterwards complained that he was 'necessitate to buckle with the enemie' despite his assessment that he was outnumbered. Just why he was 'necessitate' was not explained but there seems to have been a pretty widespread rumour that he was hustled into it by Balcarres' forwardness. At any rate all the sources agree that the battle began with a clash between his men and Lord Gordon's.

With the slope in their favour Lord Gordon's men initially threw the Covenanters back, but then were in turn brought to a stand after Balcarres committed his second squadron. Baillie himself then tried to intervene by

THE CAVALRY BATTLE AT ALFORD, 2 JULY 1645
(pages 74–75)

Alford is perhaps chiefly memorable for being the first of the Scots' civil war battles in which there was a cavalry fight of any size – which eventually decided its outcome. On the Royalist left wing Viscount Aboyne's regiment initially contented itself with an ineffectual exchange of carbine and pistol fire with Sir James Halkett's men, but over on the right wing Lord Gordon's regulars (1) came up very firmly against the two squadrons of the Earl of Balcarres' Regiment (2) – who were hardened veterans of Marston Moor. Both sides advanced into contact, fired their pistols and commenced pushing. Locked knee to knee, heavy cavalry normally attempted to ride forward and ride down the opposing regiment, theoretically 'in full career' but in reality at a steady trot. Often enough, as in the case of Aboyne's and Halkett's men, they would simply come to a halt and blaze away at a safe distance. However, if both sides kept moving and met with equal resolution, the contest quite literally turned into a pushing match remarkably similar in principle to that engaged in by pikemen. Instead of fumbling to reload their pistols or slashing ineffectively with their swords – since in any case neither side could actually reach the other – they concentrated on trying to spur or otherwise urge their horses forward with the aim of bursting apart the locked ranks in front of them (3). At first neither side had the advantage at Alford since the slope at the foot of Gallows Hill was too gentle to provide much impetus to the Royalists, beyond compensating for the fact that they were outnumbered by Balcarres' men. However, Balcarres' reserve, a locally raised squadron commanded by Sir William Forbes of Craigievar, then entered the fight by moving up and quite literally adding their weight to the press (4). Lord Gordon had no corresponding cavalry reserve and for a time was in some danger of being pushed back, but Lieutenant-Colonel Thomas Laghtnan then led forward his Irish mercenaries, ordering them to drop their pikes and muskets and fall on with their swords and dirks (5), as recalled by Gordon of Ruthven: 'colonell Nathaniell Gordoune giueing him in charge to hogh (hamstring) there horses; for they ware so many, and so well mounted, as they still raly in on one parte or other, making so many new assayes as, notwithstanding all the waliant charges they receaued by the hunder horse, who could not [be] brokin, but still charged on all quarters where there was most dangeres; yet could they not be routted till colonell McLachlen fell to worke with there horses, where-of there ware not ten of twelfe lamed when they tooke them to flight.' (Gerry Embleton)

Alford: The scene of the main battle. It was here where Baillie's infantry 'behaved themselves as became them' until overwhelmed by sheer weight of numbers and the Royalist cavalry coming in on their rear.

ordering Forbes of Craigievar's squadron to charge the rebels in flank but instead Craigievar simply moved up behind Balcarres to add his weight to the press. In the end it was the intervention of Gordon's supporting infantry which proved decisive. In just a few moments Balcarres' formation fell apart and his troopers scattered in panic.

The fighting on the other wing is rather more obscure, but the indications are that Halkett's troopers never came into contact with Aboyne's men at all. Instead both sides contented themselves with an ineffectual exchange of pistol and carbine fire until Lord Gordon, swinging right around the rear of Baillie's infantry, broke in upon Halkett's men from behind. Unfortunately, in the understandable confusion that followed Lord Gordon was killed – according to local tradition shot in the back by one of his own men, or more likely by one of Aboyne's troopers.

It was the end too for Baillie's infantry. Thus far they had held their own in a fire-fight with the rebels but, as he afterwards reported: 'Our foot stood with myselfe and behaved themselves as became them, untill the enemies horse charged in our reare, and in front we were overcharged with their foot.' George Wishart, Montrose's chaplain, also stated that 'they fought on doggedly, refusing quarter, and they were almost all of them cut down'. Substantial reinforcement drafts were certainly ordered for some of Baillie's regiments shortly afterwards and the survivors grouped together in provisional units. Halkett's Regiment for example was 'broken' and drafted into Balcarres' Regiment. However, the contemporary ballad about the battle, which relates the misfortunes of the Aberdeenshire forces with quite refreshing candour – 'They hunted us, and dunted us, and drove us here and there' – only admits to 300 dead, which may be close to the true figure.

Rebel losses may also have been high. Fraser refers to 'a considerable losse upon Montrosse his side', while Ruthven speaks of seven officers killed besides Lord Gordon, suggesting a total of 80–100 dead.

At long last Montrose had a victory that he could exploit. There was still an army under Crawford-Lindsay to the south of him but he knew that after Auldearn, Seaforth and the northern levies would not stir beyond Inverness. With Baillie's army also destroyed he was now able to move

Alford: The main cavalry battle was fought in this area, with the Royalists pushing from left to right. The Gordon Stone, supposedly marking the spot where Lord Gordon was killed, stands within an adjacent council depot.

south with his rear secure. The need for Montrose to do something to relieve the pressure upon the King was greater than ever. The King's field army had been badly beaten at Naseby in Northamptonshire a few weeks earlier.

Nevertheless it was a slow business. With his elder brother buried in Aberdeen with all due ceremony, Aboyne agreed to march south but first insisted on raising more men. In the meantime, however, he extracted a promise from Montrose that he would not commit to battle until reinforced. This rather suggests the Marquis's colleagues were by now somewhat wary of his predilection for rushing into fights without adequate reconnaissance.

Unfortunately, he then proceeded to do just that. At Fordoun in the Mearns, MacColla rejoined him with 1,400 men of the western clans and 200 of Inchbrackie's Athollmen. Encouraged by this substantial boost to his strength Montrose immediately attempted a raid on Perth. He was lucky to get away when Baillie, who had taken over Crawford-Lindsay's army, came after him and chased the Royalists back into the hills. Less lucky were the rebel camp-followers caught by Baillie's cavalry and massacred in Methven Woods.

Exasperated by his failure to catch the rebel soldiers and by what he regarded as constant political interference in military operations, Baillie then resigned as commander of the army. Only very reluctantly was he prevailed upon to serve out his notice until a replacement, Major-General Robert Monro, could be fetched home from Ireland. In the meantime Aboyne came south to rendezvous with Montrose at Dunkeld, bringing with him 400 cavalry and 800 good infantry to take part in the culminating act of the campaign.

As Montrose pushed south once more, Baillie dug in at Bridge of Earn only for the rebels to by-pass his fortified camp and head for the Mills of Forth on 11 August. Delayed first by a wayward infantry brigade that marched home to Fife without authority and then by a memorable falling out with his political masters, Baillie was slow in initiating a pursuit. He crossed Stirling Bridge on 14 August, however, and promptly had yet another acrimonious row with his superiors. By now it was clear that the rebels were heading towards Glasgow rather than Edinburgh

Kilsyth: By marching directly across country Baillie avoided the ambush which Montrose had prepared above the road. However, the 'unpassable ground' initially prevented him from exploiting the exposed Royalist flank.

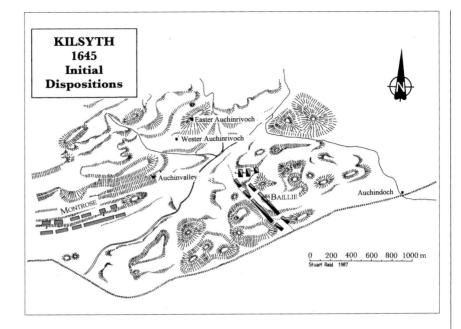

Kilsyth: By marching directly across country Baillie avoided the ambush which Montrose had prepared above the road. However, the 'unpassable ground' initially prevented him from exploiting the exposed Royalist flank.

and Baillie's scouts reported them to be encamped near Kilsyth on a high meadow overlooking the road.

KILSYTH

Next morning, learning that the rebels had not moved on, it was decided to go after them. Very sensibly, however, Baillie left the road and 'marched with the regiments through the corns and over the braes, untill the unpassible ground did hold us up. There I imbattled, where I doubt if on any quarter twenty men on a front could either have gone from us or attack us.' This was unfortunate for he was actually sitting on the rebels' left flank and so poised to inflict a memorable defeat. In the rather too confident expectation that Baillie's army would blithely march straight down the road, Montrose had drawn up his men parallel to it on the high meadow. Baillie now had the opportunity to turn the tables on his would-be ambushers but found himself frustrated by the 'unpassible' ground. Although he afterwards stressed his misgivings about the move there was no real alternative but to continue the inadvertent turning movement by striking northwards and seizing the high ground at Auchinrivoch.

Initially the move went well enough. Many secondary sources deride it as having been foolishly carried out in full view of the Royalists but, as Baillie's own very detailed account makes clear, his army was at this point in time concealed on a reverse slope. His men were therefore hidden long enough for them to get a clear start in what turned into a race for the high ground. Then everything went wrong.

Baillie had a total of some 3,500 infantry. The best of them belonged to his five regiments of regulars – Argyle's[2], Crawford-Lindsay's, Robert

Highland mercenary in long coat sketched by Köler c.1631. Wearing the long tartan coat associated with clansmen from the north of Scotland he carries both musket and bow but like the others has only a dirk instead of a broadsword.

2 This was a regular regiment, raised in the lowlands, which had been garrisoning Berwick-upon-Tweed. It should not be confused with Argyle's Highland Regiment that fought at Inverlochy.

Home's, Lauderdale's and 'three that were joyned in one'. The latter, only some 300 strong comprised the remnants of Cassillis's, Glencairn's and the Lord Chancellor's regiments. All were hardened veterans who had survived Alford or Auldearn. The remainder, however, were three newly levied regiments from Fife under the lairds of Fordell, Ferny and Cambo. All three regiments had earlier tried to disband themselves in the face of the Royalist offensive. Although they had been rounded up and fetched back again no one, understandably, had much confidence in them.

ORDER OF BATTLE
KILSYTH, 15 AUGUST 1645

ROYALISTS

Strathbogie Regiment	400
Colonel James Farquharson of Inverey's Regiment	200
Colonel William Gordon of Monymore's Regiment	200
Irish companies	500
MacColla's Lifeguard	120
Colonel Patrick Graham of Inchbrackie's Regiment	200
Western Clans	1,400

Cavalry

Viscount Aboyne's Regiment	300
Colonel Nathaniel Gordon's Regiment	80
Earl of Airlie's Regiment	80

Dragooners

Viscount Aboyne's Regiment	120
Captain John Mortimer's (Irish) Regiment	100

COVENANTERS

Marquis of Argyle's Regiment	300
Earl of Crawford-Lindsay's Regiment	400
Colonel Robert Home's Regiment	1,000
Earl of Lauderdale's Regiment	400
Lieutenant-Colonel John Kennedy's Battalion ('three … joyned in one')	300

Fife levies

Colonel James Arnot of Ferny's Regiment	400
Colonel John Henderson of Fordell's Regiment	400
Sir Thomas Morton of Cambo's Regiment	400

Cavalry

Earl of Balcarres' Regiment	300 [3]
Colonel Harie Barclay's Regiment	60

Baillie intended that his march should be screened by a composite battalion of musketeers drawn from the ranks of his regular regiments. When they broke cover a short distance to the north of the start line, however, they were spotted immediately by the rebels. At that point, to

3 Balcarres' Regiment was actually stronger than it had been at Alford as a squadron that had been detached with the Earl of Crawford-Lindsay's independent force subsequently rejoined the regiment. Balcarres also absorbed the remnants of Sir James Halkett's Regiment.

Kilsyth: Baillie's attempt to manoeuvre on to the Royalists' flank degenerated into a confused encounter battle as both sides hurried all available units into the enclosures around Auchinvalley.

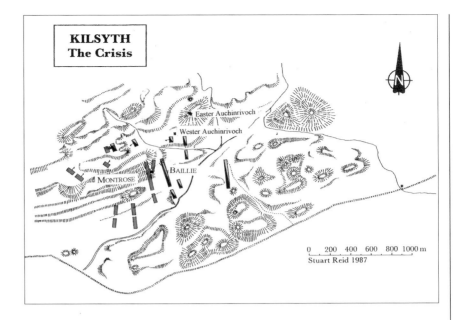

For God the king and aganist all traittouris

C ♛ R

GOD SAVE THE KING

The Strathbogie Regiment: John Spalding noted that on 15 April 1644 the Marquis of Huntly 'causit mak sum ensignes, quhair on ilk syde wes drawin ane red rampand Lion, haueing ane croun of gold above his heid, and C.R. for Carolus Rex, having this motto, FOR GOD, THE KING, AND AGAINST ALL TRAIT-TOURIS, and beneth, GOD SAVE THE KING.' The ground colour is not given, but it should logically have been yellow. Although Huntly's forces had to be temporarily disbanded shortly afterwards, the Strathbogie Regiment and its distinctive colours became a familiar sight on Scotland's battlefields.

Baillie's horror, the battalion's commander, Major John Haldane, decided that he could best carry out the spirit of his instructions by establishing himself in the farm at Auchinvalley. A rebel officer named Ewen Maclean of Treshnish immediately accepted the challenge. A spirited skirmish began around the farm enclosures and, despite Baillie's repeated orders to disengage, it soon began to escalate in intensity as MacDonald of Glengarry led up his men to reinforce Treshnish.

Recognising that, for good or ill, he had been drawn into an engagement, Baillie rode to the front with his cavalry commander, the Earl of Balcarres. In his later evidence Baillie provided both a unique insight into the sequence and nature of the orders given and a flavour of the confusion and excitement as his army, far from being helplessly swept away as it was strung out on the line of march, moved resolutely into the attack.

'He [Balcarres] asked me what he should do? I desired him to draw up his regiment on the right hand of the Earl of Lauderdale's. I gave order to Lauderdale's both by myselfe and my adjutant, to face to the right hand, and to march to the foot of the hill, then to face as they were; to Hume to follow their steps, halt when they halted, and keep distance and front with them. The Marquess [of Argyle] his Major, as I went toward him asked what he should doe? I told him, he should draw up on Hume's left hand, as he had done before. I had not ridden farr from him, when looking back, I find Hume had left the way I put him in, and wes gone at a trott, right west, in among the dykes and toward the enemy.'

First Baillie's attempt to seize the Auchinrivoch position had been sidetracked by the untimely initiative of one subordinate, now another was compounding the error by rushing to his support. Most secondary sources assume that MacColla's Highlanders overran Haldane's musketeers and then swept on to attack the rest of Baillie's army as it was strung out on the line of march. Instead, as Baillie's detailed account all-too vividly makes clear, command and control on both sides was rapidly breaking down as

81

Highland bowman wearing a yellow battle-shirt or leine. Whilst the very wide sleeves appear unconvincing they do in fact appear in contemporary illustrations. The Irish influences clearly point to his coming from one of the western clans.

the two armies rushed piecemeal into an encounter battle that neither had intended.

'I followed [Home] alse fast as I could ride,' continued Baillie; 'and meeting the Adjutant on the way, desired him he should bring up the Earl of Crafurd's regiment to Lauderdale's left hand, and cause the Generall-Major [John] Leslie draw up the regiments of Fyfe in reserve as of before; but before I could come to Hume, he and the other two regiments, to wit, the Marquess of Argyles and the three that were joyned in one, had taken in an enclosure, from whilk (the enemy being so neer) it wes impossible to bring them off.'

Instead of straggling along in a column, his army was now drawn up in three distinct bodies. Under his personal command up amongst the stone or turf-walled enclosures by Auchinvalley were some 1,600 regulars. Behind Baillie and to his right were a further 800 infantry under Major-General Holbourne and Balcarres' 300 cavalry while somewhere to his left rear were the three rather shaky Fifeshire regiments under Major-General Leslie.

Facing them were just 1,600 or so Highlanders under MacColla, pinned down for the moment on the far side of the Auchinvalley enclosures: 'The rebels foot, by this time, were approached the next dyke, on whom our musketeers made more fire than I could have wished; and therefore I did what I could, with the assistance of such of the officers as were known unto me, to make them spare their shott till the enemy should be at a nearer distance, and to keep up the musketeers with their pickes and collors, but to no great purpose.'

Nevertheless, with the Highlanders thus halted all was going to depend on what happened further to the north on what had now become Baillie's right wing. Alexander Lindsay, Earl of Balcarres, was a competent and determined officer and now he did his best to hook around into the Royalist rear. At first all that stood in his path was a small troop of cavalry commanded by a 'Captain Adjutant' Gordon. Undaunted by the odds, the Royalists immediately charged and briefly checked Balcarres' advance before the imbalance in numbers told

The remains of a civil war ravelin erected to cover the unfinished eastern wall of the Marquis of Huntly's castle at Strathbogie. It is just possible that it may have been thrown up by Montrose's forces while digging in there on the evening of 21 May 1645 but, on balance, it is unlikely that they would have had sufficient time.

against them. Just as they were on the point of being surrounded, however, Viscount Aboyne came to their aid with his personal lifeguard.

It was obviously an adventurous ride for sheering away from Harie Barclay's as yet unengaged lancers, the Royalists collided momentarily with the pikemen of Home's 'reid' regiment. They were fired on by Home's flanking musketeers before finally reaching Gordon's beleaguered troop. Unsurprisingly, by then they were in pretty poor shape and Balcarres drove them back and up on to the high ground behind Montrose's original battle-line. There at last the Covenanters were halted when Nathaniel Gordon and the Earl of Airlie counter-attacked with the main body of the Royalist cavalry. Ominously the area is still marked on modern maps as 'Slaughter Howe'. Tired and badly outnumbered, Balcarres and his men were tumbled back down the hill again and out of the fight. Worse still, the victorious Royalist troopers then turned on the now-exposed right flank of Baillie's infantry and so provided the opportunity for MacColla and his Highlanders to mount another frontal attack.

Once again, Baillie himself provided the most vivid account of what followed, relating that 'In the end the rebells leapt over the dyke, and with downe heads fell on and broke these regiments ... The present officers whom I remember were Home, his Lieutenant Colonel and Major of the Marquess's regiment, Lieutenant Colonel Campbell, and Major Menzies, Glencairne's sergeant Major, and Cassillis's Lieutenant Colonel with sundry others who behaved themselves well, and whom I saw none carefull to save themselves before the routing of the regiments. Thereafter I rode to the brae, where I found Generall Major Hollburne alone, who shew me a squadron of the rebells horsemen, who had gone by and charged the horsemen with Lieutenant-Colonell Murray and, as I supposed, did afterward rowt the Earle of Crawfurd, and these with him.'

With his front line overwhelmed by the rebel infantry, and Crawford-Lindsay's and Lauderdale's regiments dispersed by the rebel cavalry, Baillie and Holbourne 'galloped through the inclosures to have found the reserve; bot before we could come at them, they were in flight'.

Although there are no contemporary accounts of this particular episode, Baillie indirectly refers to some kind of a fight when replying to accusations that his men were so ill-prepared that they had not time to light the slow-match for their muskets before the rebels attacked: 'The fire given by the first five regiments will sufficiently answer what concerns them: and for the other three (the Fife levies), I humbly intreat your Honours to inform yourselves of Generall-Major Leslie, the adjutant, and the chief officers of these severall regiments: if they doe not satisfie yow therein, then I shall answer for myself.'

With the rebel cavalry all engaged on the northern side of the battlefield and MacColla's Highlanders fully occupied in dealing with Baillie's regulars, it must have been the Gordon foot under Farquharson of Inverey and Laghtnan and O'Cahan's Irish mercenaries who routed Leslie's Fife brigade. It was all over very quickly and the whole army completely disintegrated. Baillie and some of his officers tried to rally the fugitives at 'the brook', presumably where the road crosses a stream at Auchincloch about $1^{1}/4$ miles east of the battlefield, 'bot all in vaine'. Instead, therefore, Baillie and Holburne made their way up to Stirling where they were eventually joined by the cavalry, who were badly shaken but otherwise largely unscathed.

A good study by Köler of a Highland bowman wearing his belted plaid as a cloak, wrapped up over his shoulders. Note also the ubiquitous dirk by his side instead of a broadsword.

'Jocke'; apparently the only contemporary illustration of a Lowland Scots infantryman, with characteristic large blue bonnet, short coat open breeches. Some Royalist accounts of Auldearn mention 'helmeted men' but otherwise pikemen were unarmoured.

The magnificent (and unique) heraldic entablature above the door to Huntly Castle. The upper panels, held to have Catholic connotations, were defaced by Captain James Wallace of Monro's Regiment during the Covenanters' occupation of the castle in 1640.

This blue colour with a white saltire was captured at Dunbar, but the archaic wording of the inscription indicates that it probably belonged to Campbell of Lawers' Regiment.

Baillie's regular infantry units must have held together fairly well in the retreat and were consequently left well alone. Even the 'three that were joyned in one' survived to be individually filled out again with new recruits and sent into England, but it was a very different story with the three Fife regiments. Dissolving into a panic-stricken rabble they were pursued for miles by the exultant clansmen and hundreds ruthlessly cut down. Indeed, it was said that for years afterwards dozens of boats rotted at their moorings in the little ports along the Fife coast, their crews dead at Kilsyth. In the longer term the slaughter also contributed to the myth of Highland savagery and so, in turn, paved the way for the later victories over other Scots soldiers at Killiecrankie and Prestonpans.

Rebel casualties are unknown, but as they remained on the battlefield for another two days it can safely be surmised that they too had suffered heavy losses in what all the contemporary accounts agree had been very heavy fighting. Be that as it may, notwithstanding the beating they had just dealt out, they showed no inclination whatever to follow what remained of Baillie's army to Stirling. Instead, just as after every other victory, Montrose chose to move off in a diametrically opposite direction. Somewhere to the south of him there was another contingent of Covenanters under the Earl of Lanark. Opinion is divided as to whether Baillie knew they were close at hand when he fought at Kilsyth. While he never suggested that disaster could have been averted by joining with Lanark first, his immediate impulse after rallying the army at Stirling was to march south and rendezvous with the Earl in Clydesdale. Unfortunately his cavalry were so demoralised that they flatly refused. Oddly enough, although Lanark himself fled to Berwick on hearing the news of the battle, at least one of his regiments remained in the field. Led by a tough professional named Sir John Browne, they harassed the rebels sufficiently for Sir John to be awarded £100 sterling 'In thankful remembrance of good service with his dragoons against the rebels since 15th August last.'

Just what that service was does not appear but he no doubt did his best to curb the rebels' descent into banditry. Glasgow was taken without opposition, but the clans were disappointed by Montrose's refusal to let them sack the city. Nor did the 'storm-money' promised in lieu materialise and when Montrose, anxious to remove his men from temptation, withdrew to a camp at Bothwell they took to marauding instead and deserted in droves. There was perhaps some justification for a cavalry raid on Edinburgh mounted by Nathaniel Gordon, but little for a much larger raid on Kilmarnock and the towns along the Ayrshire coast led by MacColla. On 2 or 3 September MacColla left for good, taking all the remaining Highlanders with him, on his ultimately doomed attempt to re-establish MacDonald hegemony in the Isles.

With his army melting away around him as never before, Montrose bestirred himself into marching on Edinburgh. After only the first day, however, Aboyne took his Gordons north, leaving Montrose with barely 500 Irish infantry and not much more than 100 cavalry. At this point Montrose should also have re-crossed the Forth, but instead seems to have decided that he must try to join the King in England at all costs, and so continued on his way to Edinburgh.

He never reached the capital. Learning that the plague – almost certainly typhus brought back by the army from the camps in England – was raging there, he instead turned south at Dalkeith, hoping to raise large numbers of cavalry in the borders. At first the signs were promising. The Marquis of Douglas joined him at Galashiels on 7 September with around 1,000 moss-troopers, but neither the Earl of Home nor the Earl of Roxburgh appeared at Kelso the next day. By 10 September he was at Jedburgh, poised to move south into England, when disturbing news reached him. Lieutenant-General David Leslie had passed through Berwick on 6 September with at least four regiments of infantry and six regiments of cavalry.

Abandoning for the moment any thought of crossing the border, the rebels headed west, probably with the idea of evading Leslie and regaining the hills by way of Clydesdale. On the afternoon of 12 September they reached Selkirk and while Montrose and all too many of his officers found comfortable quarters in the burgh, the greater number of the cavalry camped just to the west on the flat expanse of Philiphaugh and the infantry bivouacked in a nearby wood. As usual they were camping 'commodiously', which was unfortunate for unbeknown to them Leslie was approaching fast.

Intent on saving Edinburgh, Leslie had been hastening along the coast road (now the A1), but at the tiny village of Gladsmuir on 11 September he received word that the rebels were in fact lurking somewhere to the south of him. At least a part of Lord Coupar's Regiment of Foot may already have been mounted and taking them along with his own cavalry, and two other regiments that joined him at Gladsmuir, he immediately set off in pursuit, leaving the rest of his infantry trailing behind.

The following night he ran into a rebel outpost in the village of Sunderland a little way to the north of Selkirk. Quite unsuspecting, the Royalists were literally caught napping and after a short, sharp fight only the commander, Charteris of Amisfield, and two or three of his men got away. In itself this was bad enough but, quite incredibly, when they reached Selkirk they were assumed to have been involved in a drunken brawl. Amisfield's report that they had been attacked by Leslie's men was dismissed out of hand and no attempt was made to rouse the army. Undisturbed therefore, Leslie and his men appear to have spent the rest of the night in the valley of the Tweed between Linglie Hill and Meigle Hill, just a little upstream from Sunderland.

Having left the majority of his infantry behind, Leslie had just over six cavalry regiments – his own, the Earl of Leven's, John Middleton's, Lord Kirkcudbright's, Lord Montgomery's and the Earl of Dalhousie's – together with 40 troopers of Colonel Harie Barclay's Regiment (the latter two units joined him at Gladsmuir). According to pay warrants these totalled some 3,000 men. In addition, he also had some 400 men of Colonel Hugh Fraser's Dragoons – reputedly one of the best units in the Scots army – and as many as 700 of Lord Coupar's Regiment of Foot, though it is perhaps questionable whether he had been able to find enough nags to mount all of them.

THE BATTLE OF PHILIPHAUGH

Ironically, the following morning dawned grey and misty and, had any notice been taken of Amisfield's warning, the rebels might have been able to escape under cover of the fog. Instead they spent a lazy morning waiting for it to clear while all the time Leslie and his troopers were

This gentleman is probably not a Highlander but a laird from North-East Scotland, wearing a combination of low-country and Highland clothes. He would be equally at home on foot or horseback, speaking Gaelic or Scots.

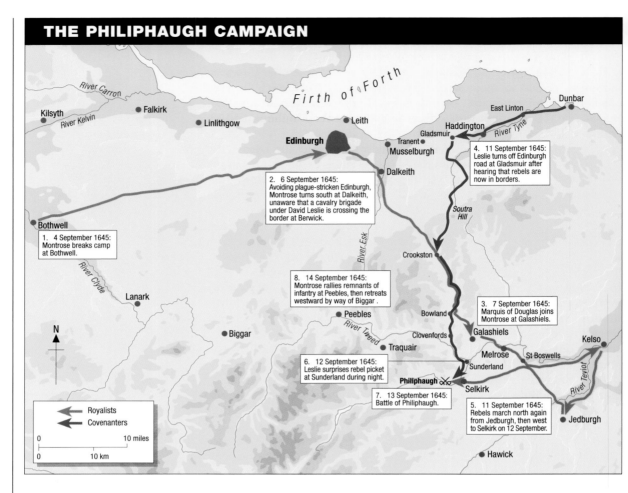

Kilsyth
River Carron
River Kelvin
Falkirk
Linlithgow
Firth of Forth
Leith
Dunbar
East Linton
River Tyne
Haddington
Gladsmuir
Edinburgh
Tranent
Musselburgh
Dalkeith

4. 11 September 1645:
Leslie turns off Edinburgh
road at Gladsmuir after
hearing that rebels are
now in borders.

2. 6 September 1645:
Avoiding plague-stricken Edinburgh,
Montrose turns south at Dalkeith,
unaware that a cavalry brigade
under David Leslie is crossing the
border at Berwick.

Soutra
Hill

Bothwell

1. 4 September 1645:
Montrose breaks camp
at Bothwell.

River Clyde

River Esk

Crookston

8. 14 September 1645:
Montrose rallies remnants of
infantry at Peebles, then retreats
westward by way of Biggar .

3. 7 September 1645:
Marquis of Douglas joins
Montrose at Galashiels.

Lanark

Peebles
Bowland

N

Biggar
River Tweed
Clovenfords
Galashiels
Kelso
Traquair
Melrose
St Boswells
Sunderland

6. 12 September 1645:
Leslie surprises rebel picket
at Sunderland during night.

Philiphaugh
Selkirk
River Teviot

7. 13 September 1645:
Battle of Philiphaugh.

5. 11 September 1645:
Rebels march north again
from Jedburgh, then west
to Selkirk on 12 September.

Jedburgh

Hawick

Royalists
Covenanters

0   10 miles
0   10 km

closing in. Legend has it that Montrose was still at breakfast when his scoutmaster, Captain Blackadder, crashed through the door 'in a great fright' to announce that Leslie was at hand, but Leslie's official report unequivocally states that he attacked at 10.00am.

Be that as it may, Montrose flung himself on to the first horse he could catch and galloped across to Philiphaugh where he found 'all in uproar and confusion'. The large body of cavalry encamped there was not only untrained and inexperienced but most of their officers, like Montrose, had taken themselves off to find beds in Selkirk the night before. Consequently the troopers were now scattered all over the haugh in loose bodies and making no attempt to form a battle-line. Even the veteran Irish, recognising perhaps that the battle was already lost, were in some disorder with a great many of them intent only on saving their own baggage.

The result was that Laghtnan and O'Cahan could only bring up about 200 infantry, less than half their number. At least, 'According to their usual manner they had made choice of a most advantageous ground wherein they had entrenched themselves, having upon one hand an impassable ditch and on the other dikes and hedges, and where these were not strong enough they further fortified them by casting up ditches and lined their hedges with musketeers.'

This blue cavalry cornet with gold lettering, captured at Dunbar, bears the motto of the Forbes family and may have been carried by one of the Aberdeenshire units which fought against Montrose.

From this description it would appear that the Irish were drawn up facing north with their left flank anchored on the Philhope Burn, their front covered by agricultural walls and ditches and the gap between their right flank and the river Ettrick held by the small body of veteran cavalry under Nathaniel Gordon and Lord Ogilvy.

With a very comfortable superiority in numbers, Leslie divided his army in two at the Linglie Burn about 1/2 mile north of Selkirk. One wing, led by Lieutenant-Colonel James Agnew of Lord Kirkcudbright's Regiment, crossed the River Ettrick and cleared Selkirk itself, capturing or chasing off those officers who had not been as quick off the mark as Montrose. The remainder of Leslie's men, according to a reliable local ballad tradition, swung around the base of Linglie Hill and went straight at the rebels.

In a vain attempt to delay this advance Nathaniel Gordon led his troopers forward and engaged Leslie's skirmishers in an exchange of carbine and pistol fire, but badly outnumbered they were driven in within a quarter of an hour. To cover their retreat either Laghtnan or O'Cahan led forward a body of musketeers. This in itself is sufficient indication of how desperate the situation was becoming. Almost at once, however, they were 'forced by ours to retreat in great disorder', presumably by Lord Coupar's now dismounted infantry.

ORDER OF BATTLE
PHILIPHAUGH, 13 SEPTEMBER 1645

ROYALISTS

Irish companies	500

Cavalry

Colonel Nathaniel Gordon's Regiment	60
Earl of Airlie's Regiment	60
Marquis of Douglas's levies	1,000

COVENANTERS[4]

Earl of Leven's Horse	550
David Leslie's Horse	550
John Middleton's Horse	400
Lord Kirkcudbright's Horse	600
Lord Montgomery's Horse	470
Harie Barclay's Horse	40
Earl of Dalhousie's Horse	330
Hugh Fraser's Dragoons	400
Lord Coupar's Foot	700

James Graham, Marquis of Montrose as depicted in the frontispiece to the first (1647) edition of the very influential biography penned by his personal chaplain.

After these preliminaries there then seems to have been a pause before the battle began in earnest, perhaps because Leslie was still trying to

---

4 For once the numbers in each regiment can be established with reasonable precision since a grateful Government awarded a bounty to all those who fought at Philiphaugh.

develop the rebel position in the fog. The front between the enclosures occupied by the rebel infantry and the River Ettrick was relatively narrow. When Leslie moved forward again he could, therefore, send forward only one regiment at a time. His first attack was repulsed but when the rebels counter-charged for a second time they found themselves cut off and tried to escape northwards. By this time it was about noon. Montrose and his cavalry commander, the Earl of Crawford, had succeeded in patching together a second line with the border levies. Leslie ignored them, however, and instead wheeled to his right and 'charging very desperately upon the head of his own regiment, broke the body of the enemy's Foot, after which they all went in confusion and disorder'. Matters were not helped when Lieutenant-Colonel Agnew, having cleared Selkirk, crossed the Ettrick and attacked the remaining rebel cavalry who fled in all directions without putting up a fight.

Amidst the confusion, Montrose's adjutant, Stewart, managed to rally about 100 of the Irish at Philiphaugh Farm but surrendered after a vicious little fight that left half of them dead. With that the battle ended, but not the killing. Coldly announcing that quarter had only been promised to Stewart, O'Cahan and Laghtnan, Leslie proceeded to have all his prisoners shot. The numerous camp followers were also murdered, either then or over the next few days, but otherwise the rebels escaped surprisingly lightly.

Most of the cavalry escaped simply because they were able to run away faster, especially since most of them were local men, but at least half of the Irish infantry also got away. According to Wishart, 250 of them rejoined Montrose afterwards, probably at Peebles where he spent the night. Next day he crossed the Clyde, picking up some 200 Horse at the ford, and then swung north across the Forth and the Earn, taking refuge in Atholl by 19 September.

Having won a neat little victory, Leslie displayed little interest in pursuing the rebels and instead retraced his steps northwards to Haddington and then to Edinburgh. His seeming complacency was justified by events. Judged purely in material terms the rebels had escaped comparatively lightly from the fight at Philiphaugh. True, Montrose lost a couple of hundred of his veteran Irish mercenaries, but Leslie's main achievement was in preventing him from recruiting a fresh army in the borders to replace the Gordons. The importance of this achievement was underlined in the months that followed.

THE LAST CAMPAIGN

At Dunkeld Montrose was rejoined by Inchbrackie but appeals to MacColla went unanswered and so he marched northwards with some 800 infantry and 200 cavalry to try to link up with the Gordons again. Instead he found himself in the middle of a local civil war that had little to do with national politics and everything to do with deep-seated family rivalries.

Returning home after Kilsyth, Aboyne had quite fortuitously surprised and captured the entire Committee of War for the north-eastern sheriffdoms and then followed this up by installing William Gordon of Arradoul as governor of Aberdeen and demanding that the burgh militia

DEO ET VICTRICIBUS ARMIS

This rather macabre black colour was made for Montrose in Holland or Denmark and carried by his mercenary infantry at the battle of Carbisdale in 1650. The severed head, dripping blood, is that of King Charles, copied here from a contemporary woodcut.

be mobilised as a garrison. Unsurprisingly this led to Major-General John Middleton being sent north with 800 men of his own and Lord Montgomery's Regiments and he re-occupied the burgh at the end of the month. Although Middleton was understandably wary of venturing further with his little brigade, his presence provided sufficient impetus for a revival of pro-Government activity in Aberdeenshire under the Master of Forbes.

It was against this unpromising background that Montrose re-appeared and persuaded Aboyne to meet him at Drumminor Castle with some 1,500 infantry and as much as 500 cavalry under his wild younger brother, Lord Lewis Gordon. However, the Marquis 'fynding himselfe now stronge eneugh to giue his enemies a day' (i.e. strong enough to give battle), announced that he intended to march south again rather than confront Middleton, who by then was lying at Turriff. Aboyne very reluctantly agreed but then Montrose rather tactlessly put Lord Lewis Gordon under the command of the Earl of Crawford. Viewed objectively the appointment of Crawford, an experienced professional soldier, to lead the Royalist cavalry was a sensible enough move. Lord Lewis Gordon not only refused to acknowledge his authority, however, but proceeded to assert his independence by undertaking an unauthorised raid on one of Middleton's outposts at Kintore.

The raid was spectacularly successful. Middleton's men, considerably outnumbered, fell back to Turriff in such a panic that Middleton in turn fled northwards to Banff. There he was uncomfortably close to Strathbogie and this was sufficient excuse for Lord Lewis Gordon to return there. This in turn left Montrose with insufficient cavalry support for his proposed march southwards and so he reluctantly turned back to Alford where Aboyne also left him and returned to Strathbogie. Left with just Inchbrackie's men and the last remaining Irish mercenaries, he moved over the mountains to Dunkeld and then, with the aid of a few recruits levied by Robertson of Inver, he tried to threaten Glasgow. This move was aimed at least in part at saving the lives of the Royalist officers captured at Philiphaugh. However, Leslie's cavalry successfully kept him in the hills, O'Cahan, Laghtnan and Nathaniel Gordon were all hanged and, at the end of October, Montrose at last admitted defeat and trailed northwards to make his peace with the Marquis of Huntly.

Since the collapse of his own uprising in April of the previous year, Huntly had been in hiding in Strathnavar in the far north of Scotland. Now he was back and, while he was willing to put old differences aside for the present and work with Montrose, he made it very plain that he would do so as an ally rather than a subordinate. Moreover it also soon became clear that he regarded himself as the senior partner. He was operating on his own turf, by far the greater number of the Royalist troops owed him their personal allegiance and, in any case, Montrose was widely regarded as far too reckless and perhaps even more than a little unstable. This was the real legacy of Philiphaugh.

Ironically, Montrose had raised the rebellion in the first place to relieve pressure on his beleaguered King. The crushing Parliamentarian victory at Naseby in June, which had first drawn him south and then led him to undertake the disastrous march into the borders, now meant that sufficient Scots regulars could at last be released to deal with him. As winter approached, Glasgow was heavily garrisoned and fortified, and a strong line of outposts established along the Forth crossings. Dalhousie's Regiment was based on Stirling while Lord Montgomery's and Colonel Hugh Fraser's Dragoons lay in Clackmannanshire. Lord Kirkcudbright's Regiment was pushed forward to re-occupy Baillie's old fortified camp at Bridge of Earn, from where contact could be maintained with both the Dundee garrison and with the Earl of Moray's Foot, who were watching the Highland passes out of Atholl.

Further north, however, only Inverness was still in the Government's hands and so, at the beginning of January 1646, Colonel Harie Barclay arrived in Aberdeen with his own regiments of horse and dragoons, Colonel Robert Montgomery's Horse and two regular infantry regiments that had come north with Leslie – Colonel William Stewart's and Viscount Kenmure's. There they halted until the spring, while the battered but indefatigable Aberdeenshire levies were re-organised into a regiment of horse under the Master of Forbes and a regiment of foot under Colonel George Forbes of Mill Buie.

This important work was carried out without any interference since the greater part of the remaining Royalists were now on the far side of the river Spey. There Montrose was vainly trying to raise a new army while the Gordons engaged in a petty round of raid and counter-raid against their neighbours. Only the Earl of Crawford, based at Banff, presented any threat to the growing concentration at Aberdeen. At first he made life distinctly uncomfortable for Barclay with a series of raids pushed down Deeside by Farquharson of Inverey and from Fyvie Castle by Captain Blackadder. Eventually Barclay decided enough was enough and riposted with an even heavier raid on Banff that sent the rebels tumbling back across the Spey.

By the end of April relations between the Royalist commanders had deteriorated to the extent that Huntly and Montrose were operating independently of each other. Montrose embarked on a futile siege of Inverness. It was also reckless as Major-General John Middleton had come north to supersede Barclay and was then lying at Banff with a cavalry brigade and Mill Buie's Foot. Huntly, on the other hand, having allowed his infantry to winter at home, had not yet concentrated his forces and was unable to cover the siege when Middleton suddenly lunged forward with his cavalry. Wishart subsequently accused the Gordons of treachery and alleged that Montrose's rearguard, two troops of Irish dragooners commanded by captains Mortimer and McDonnell, were purposely decoyed away by Lord Lewis Gordon. Ruthven, on the other hand, explicitly denies the charge and accuses them of being negligent, which is altogether more convincing.

Whatever the truth of the matter, Middleton suddenly crossed the Spey, pausing only long enough at Elgin to feed and water his horses before pushing straight on through the night to Inverness. Having marched no

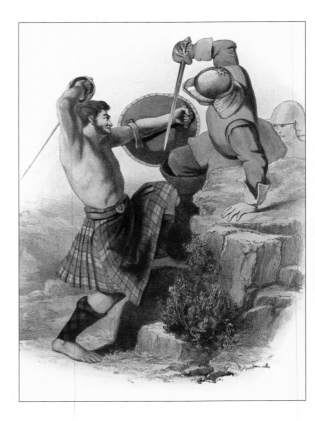

A splendidly anachronistic yet evocative study of a Highland swordsman by MacIan.

fewer than 45 miles with no more than this single halt he took the Royalists completely by surprise. Alerted only by Middleton's trumpets, Montrose's men abandoned their guns and fled westwards without attempting to fight. Had they done so, Middleton might well have been defeated as both men and horses must have been utterly exhausted, but the deliberately sounded trumpet blast was enough.

With that the campaign was all but over. After clinging on for a few days Montrose swung to the south and took refuge in Speyside while Huntly, displaying unwonted energy, struck south and stormed Aberdeen on 14 May 1646. 'It was thought' said one chronicler, 'to be one of the hottest pieces of service that happened since this unnatural war began, both in regard to the eagerness of the pursuers and valour of the defenders.' It was also seven years to the day since the civil wars had begun with the Gordons' victory over the Covenanters at Turriff in 1639. Three weeks later it was officially all over when word arrived from the King ordering the last of his forces to lay down their arms.

After protracted negotiations, Montrose accordingly surrendered to Middleton at Rattray near Blairgowrie on 30 July and then fled abroad. After four years he would return again, with a motley army of exiles and mercenaries, only to be ambushed at Carbisdale on 27 April 1650 and hanged in Edinburgh a month later. Ironically enough, hanged with him was Sir John Hurry who had fought against him at Auldearn, only to change sides and lead the Royalist cavalry at Carbisdale.

THE BATTLEFIELDS TODAY

As will be readily apparent from the numerous photographs, Montrose's battlefields are very accessible and are still to a surprising degree relatively untouched.

Aberdeen: Notwithstanding its having been completely swallowed up by the expansion of the city early in the 19th century the scene of the Craibstane Rout, or battle of the Justice Mills, can still be visited with advantage and is, quite literally, two minutes away from the western end of the main thoroughfare, Union Street. A short walk down Bon Accord Terrace will take you to the Craibstane and the road junction at the top of the Hardgate where the hardest fighting took place. Astonishingly enough, as can be seen from the photographs, much of the battlefield is still quite open and it is very easy to read the topography.

Following the Hardgate down into the valley and up the other side will bring you on to Willowbank, where Montrose originally deployed his forces and following it for another mile or so will bring you to the old Brig o' Dee, the scene of Montrose's first victory in 1639.

At the other, eastern, end of Union Street is the Castlegate or principal market place, which was very usefully described at the time as large enough to draw up two regiments of foot. Huntly's storming in 1646 culminated in a cavalry battle here. Behind the baronial pile of the former Salvation Army Citadel is a surviving bastion of a stone fort built by Cromwell's forces in the 1650s.

Inverlochy: The route followed by the Royalist army south across the hills from Kilchummin (Fort Augustus) is totally unspoiled and, by any standards, spectacular but not for the faint-hearted. The barn at Keppoch, where the advance guard rested after evicting one of Argyle's outposts, appears to be the original structure standing in 1645 although its thatch has long since been replaced by the ubiquitous corrugated iron. As for the battlefield itself, trees and an aluminium smelter largely obscure Montrose's original position by Torlundy outside modern Fort William, but the suprisingly compact ruins of Inverlochy Castle may still be viewed on the other side of the valley. The area around it, where most of the fighting took place, is now a golf course.

Auldearn: The modern village is obviously somewhat larger than in 1645 but, although it has to some extent spilled down into the once marshy 'bottom', most of the modern development has spread eastwards leaving the battlefield and, in particular, Garlic Hill, virtually untouched. It is unique amongst all of Montrose's battles in being signposted, but interpretation and visitor facilities are limited to a small car-park at the foot of the castle hill and a frequently vandalised map, maintained by

As an aside it is worth having a look at this surviving bastion and trace of a fort erected on the old castle hill in Aberdeen by Cromwellian forces in the 1650s – one of the country's few surviving examples of a Civil War fortification.

the National Trust for Scotland, on top of it. As in 1645, the castle hill presents the best vantage-point from which to see most of the battlefield. It is also important to drop down into the bottom, however, in order to appreciate the tactical importance of Garlic Hill and the way in which it dominates the battlefield. The hill itself has been cleared of gorse and is now farmed but, if an opportunity presents itself, it is well worth climbing. Not only does it provide a quite different perspective, it is also immediately apparent how the relatively low ridges on either side masked the eventual Royalist counter-attack. Similarly it is instructive to compare the attackers' view of the village from the top of the hill with the very different view from the marshy bottom immediately below – although the ground is now much drier the stream is easy to find.

Alford: The battlefield is once again completely untouched, other than now being divided up by dry-stone field boundaries. All the action took place on the gentle slopes and open fields between Gallows Hill and the present village. There are, however, no signposts or interpretative facilities so a good map is essential. The river Don is now spanned by a narrow bridge at Mountgarrie but the ford used by Baillie in his advance to contact can easily be found just a few yards upstream.

Kilsyth: Frustratingly, the battlefield of Kilsyth, although otherwise undeveloped, is partially submerged by a reservoir constructed to service the Forth and Clyde Canal early in the 19th century. Nevertheless, it is still worth a visit. It lies on the north side of the A803 and is best approached along that road from Stirling. Although Baillie struck off the road to avoid the rather inept ambush prepared for him it is best to stay on the road as far as the small village of Banton and then turn northwards along a very minor road to the even smaller village of Kelvinhead. Baillie almost certainly deployed his army along the line of this road, below the crest that screened him from the rebel army on the other side of a shallow valley now filled by the reservoir. Despite the intrusion of this body of water it is very easy to see why Baillie reckoned the ground immediately to his front to be 'impassable'.

BIBLIOGRAPHY

Historians have traditionally based their study of this campaign on Wishart's adulatory (and quite untrustworthy) biography of Montrose but a very different picture emerges from other sources. The best accounts of Auldearn come from Fraser for the Covenanters and Gordon of Ruthven for the Royalists. The astonishingly detailed formal evidence provided by Lieutenant-General William Baillie to the inquiry into the defeats at Alford and Kilsyth is found amongst the Letters and Journals of his kinsman, Robert Baillie. The best analysis of Philiphaugh comes from Colonel Fitzwilliam Eliott in his study of border ballads. Not only was he intimately familiar with the ground but, having commanded a mounted infantry brigade in South Africa, he had a very lively appreciation of how much space was occupied by cavalry units and just where they could and could not go.

Baillie, Robert, *Letters and Journals,* 3 vols (Bannatyne Club, 1841–42)

Bariffe, William, *Militarie Discipline, or the Young Artillery-man* (Partisan Press, Leigh on Sea, 1989)

Cowan, Edward, *Montrose, For Covenant and King* (London, 1977)

Eliott, Fitzwilliam, *The Trustworthiness of Border Ballads* (1906)

Fraser, James, *Chronicles of the Frasers; The Wardlaw Manuscript* (Scottish History Society, 1906)

Gordon of Rothiemay, James, *History of Scots Affairs*, 3 vols (Spalding Club, 1841)

Gordon of Sallagh, Gilbert, *Continuation of a History of the Earldom of Sutherland* (Edinburgh, 1813)

Gordon of Ruthven, Patrick, *A Short Abridgement of Britane's Distemper* (Spalding Club, 1844)

Gordon, William, *The History on the Ancient, Noble and Illustrious Family of Gordon* (Edinburgh, 1727)

Marren, Peter, *Grampian Battlefields* (Aberdeen, 1990)

Reid, Stuart, *The Campaigns of Montrose* (Edinburgh, 1990)

Reid, Stuart, *Highland Clansman* (Osprey, 1997)

Reid, Stuart, *Scots Armies of the English Civil War* (Osprey, 1999)

Reid, Stuart, *All the Kings Armies* (Staplehurst, 1998)

Reid, Stuart, *Highlander* (London, 2000)

Spalding, John, *Memorialls of the Trubles in Scotland 1627–1645*, 2 vols (Spalding Club, 1850–51)

Stevenson, David, *The Scottish Revolution 1637–44* (London, 1973)

Stevenson, David, *Revolution and Counter-revolution in Scotland 1644–51* (London, 1977)

Stevenson, David, *Alasdair MacColla and the Highland Problem in the 17th century* (Edinburgh, 1980)

Stevenson, David, *Scottish Covenanters and Irish Confederates* (Belfast, 1981)

Terry, C.S., *Papers Relating to the Army of the Solemn League and Covenant*, 2 vols (Scottish History Soc., 1917–18)

Wishart, George, *Memoirs of James, Marquis of Montrose, 1639–1650* (London, 1893)

INDEX

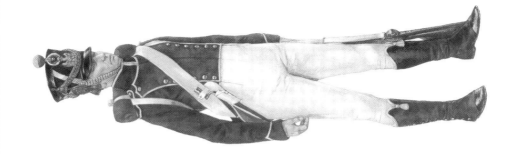

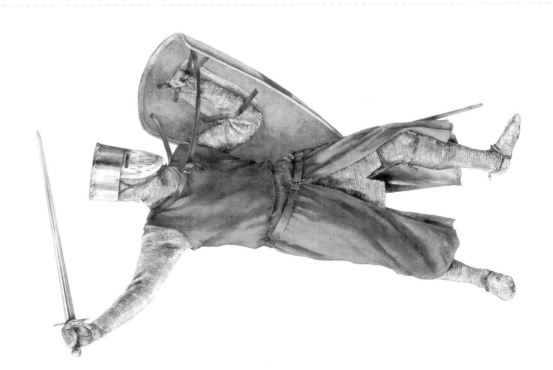

OSPREY
PUBLISHING

www.ospreypublishing.com

call our telephone hotline
for a free information pack

USA & Canada: 1-800-826-6600
UK, Europe and rest of world call:
+44 (0) 1933 443 863

Young Guardsman
Figure taken from *Warrior 22:
Imperial Guardsman 1799–1815*
Published by Osprey
Illustrated by Christa Hook

Knight, c.1190
Figure taken from *Warrior 1: Norman Knight 950 – 1204 AD*
Published by Osprey
Illustrated by Christa Hook

POSTCARD

Related titles & companion series from Osprey

FORTRESS (FOR)
**Design, technology and history of key fortresses,
strategic positions and defensive systems**
Contact us for more details – see below

ESSENTIAL HISTORIES (ESS)
**Concise overviews of major wars
and theatres of war**
Contact us for more details – see below

To order any of these titles, or for more information on Osprey Publishing, contact:
Osprey Direct (UK)   *Tel:* +44 (0)1933 443863   *Fax:* +44 (0)1933 443849   *E-mail:* info@ospreydirect.co.uk
Osprey Direct (USA) c/o MBI Publishing   *Toll-free:* 1 800 826 6600   *Phone:* 1 715 294 3345
Fax: 1 715 294 4448   *E-mail:* info@ospreydirectusa.com
www.ospreypublishing.com

Accounts of history's greatest conflicts, detailing the command strategies, tactics and battle experiences of the opposing forces throughout the crucial stages of each campaign.

Full colour battlescenes

3-dimensional 'bird's eye view' maps

Illustrations

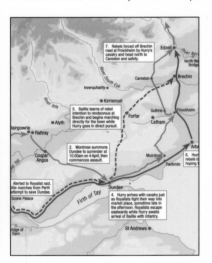

Maps

Auldearn 1645

The Marquis of Montrose' Scottish campaign

In August 1644, at the height of the First English Civil War, James Graham, Marquis of Montrose, raised the standard of Royalist rebellion in Scotland In a single year he won a string of remarkable victories with his army of Irish mercenaries and Highland clansmen. His victory at Auldearn, the centrepiece of his campaign, was won only after a day-long struggle and heavy casualties on both sides. This book details the remarkable sequence of victorie at Tibbermore, Aberdeen, Inverlochy, Auldearn and Kilsyth that left Montrose briefl in the ascendant in Scotland. However, his decisive defeat and surrender at Philiphaugh finally crushed the Royalist cause in Scotland.

OSPREY
PUBLISHING

www.ospreypublishing.com

ISBN 1-84176-679-8

9 781841 766799